African American RAILROAD WORKERS
OF ROANOKE

African American
RAILROAD WORKERS
OF ROANOKE
ORAL HISTORIES OF THE NORFOLK & WESTERN

SHEREE SCARBOROUGH

Charleston London

THE
History
PRESS

Published by The History Press
Charleston, SC 29403
www.historypress.net

First published 2014

Manufactured in the United States

ISBN 978.1.62619.504.2

Library of Congress CIP data applied for.

*For those who shared their stories with me,
especially the Reverend Carl T. Tinsley (1933–2013)
and John W. Divers (1918–2014).*

CONTENTS

CONTENTS

Foreword

PIECES OF A LARGER MOSAIC

During the early summer of 1948, my mother took me on a train trip to New York City. I was five years old. We boarded a Norfolk & Western passenger train at the depot in Buena Vista, Virginia, on a pleasant summer evening. There are not many things that I remember about that evening because far too many years have passed. Yet the excitement of watching that large train speed into the depot has always been one of my more pleasant memories. I also vaguely remember the conductor in his dark uniform and the porter in his starched white jacket. The conductor was white, and the porter was black. Whether or not, at five years of age, I remembered that one was black and the other white is unimportant. During the Jim Crow era, jobs on southern railroads were clearly segregated by race. In part, *African American Railroad Workers of Roanoke: Oral Histories of the Norfolk and Western* tells the story of black railroad employees in Roanoke, Virginia, as they remember it.

The train that I boarded with my mother would have originated in Roanoke, about forty-five miles south of Buena Vista. Roanoke is a post–Civil War boomtown that attracted many new residents during the last two decades of the nineteenth century. Its rapid growth was remarkable; by 1900, it ranked as Virginia's third-largest city. In 1890, its total population was 16,159, 70 percent of whom were white.[1] Its African American residents

---

1. Rand Dotson, *Roanoke, Virginia, 1882–1912: Magic City of the New South* (Knoxville: University of Tennessee Press, 2007), 67–68.

began arriving during the 1880s and 1890s and represented the city's second-largest community. Only menial labor jobs were available to them. Black men were mostly day laborers, while black women were mostly domestic servants. Historian Rand Dotson has observed that black families lived mostly below the subsistence level, but the wages they earned in Roanoke gave them far better options than sharecropping.[2]

Black labor on southern railroads dates to the antebellum era, when enslaved people toiled to construct tracks. Railroad companies had two options: renting or owning enslaved people. They did both. Constructing tracks was backbreaking and grueling work during the years prior to the Civil War, and it would remain so during the twentieth century. After 1876, some southern railroad companies in the lower South would move from slavery to convict leasing as a means of obtaining an abundant supply of cheap laborers. Such workers were no more than slaves. Many of the convicts were guilty only of breaking the South's vagrancy laws. These were statutes that entrapped out-of-work black men. Convict leasing provided income for southern states and cheap labor for the railroads and was less humane than slavery.[3] The living and working conditions of these men were deplorable. Fortunately, Norfolk & Western was not built by convicts.

The significance of jobs with Norfolk & Western is that the company paid salaries to blacks, no matter how menial those early jobs were. Pay was relatively low, but the work was steady because of the boom in southern railroad construction that began in 1879. Within the first ten years, southern railroads increased from 16,605 miles to 39,108 miles, thanks in large part to the investment of more than $150 million in capital by northern and foreign entrepreneurs.[4] The Norfolk & Western Railroad, in like manner, attracted thousands of northern investors to the Roanoke area, absorbed other railroads and more than tripled the miles of its tracks, thus ensuring employment for lots of day laborers.[5] Following the depression of 1893,

2. Dotson, *Roanoke*, 105–07.

3. Leon F. Litwack, *Trouble in Mind: Black Southerners in the Age of Jim Crow* (New York: Alfred A. Knopf, 1998), 271–72.

4. C. Vann Woodward, *The Origins of The New South, 1877–1913* (Baton Rouge: Louisiana State University Press and the Littlefield Fund for Southern History, University of Texas, 1971), 120.

5. Dotson, *Roanoke*, 59.

Rail gangs used hand tools such as pickaxes, shovels, tie tongs and mallets to repair and replace track. *Norfolk Southern Corporation.*

Norfolk & Western prospered. It transported an increased amount of coal, moving approximately 3 million tons from Virginia mines. The company purchased over three hundred locomotives and thousands of freight cars known as coal hoppers. It also served an impressive number of passengers. During the early 1890s, it boasted receipts for the sale of more than 2 million passenger tickets. The company's gross intake dramatically increased, exceeding $10 million in the 1890s.[6]

In spite of economic progress, Norfolk & Western was a southern company that was bound by Jim Crow laws and customs. And so was the booming city of Roanoke. Norfolk & Western jobs continued to be very important to workers and their families but were clearly defined by race. Restriction of job opportunities by race was worst, however, in the North and other regions. Historian Eric Arnesen has written that railroads had "something of a labor aristocracy" that placed engineers and conductors at the top. He notes that skills and ethnicity defined who held those privileged positions. Their wages, authority and autonomy placed them at the top, where their compensation and independence was impressive. Engineers had the greatest

---

6. Dotson, *Roanoke*, 61–62.

responsibility and had to master the technology and direct the train's physical operations. Conductors, who ranked second, supervised the brakemen and porters. They were also responsible for the freight. Locomotive firemen and brakemen performed vital but dangerous tasks and occupied a lower place in this labor aristocracy than did the engineers and conductors.[7] Only the porters were black.

As late as the 1950s and 1960s, some trades among American railway workers continued to be racially and ethnically homogenous. Locomotive engineers and conductors were white. Northern and western white men, who had long been entrenched in these jobs, insisted on a strict color line that effectively prevented competition from blacks or other racial and ethnic groups. To some extent, blacks outside of the South worked in dual roles as brakemen and porters. In the South, however, the situation was a bit different. Southern railroads offered a wider variety of jobs to black workers. By the beginning of the twentieth century, blacks held the majority of firemen and brakemen jobs on many of the southern lines. Both were essential jobs that entailed hard work and risk of bodily harm.[8]

During the twentieth century, railroad brotherhoods or labor unions evolved. Initially, these groups barred black membership and worked to prevent blacks and various ethnic groups from competing for the "white jobs" that paid better. The southern states in general and southern corporations in particular were hostile to unions. Typically, unions had little influence in the South, although they had many good features. Most importantly, they attempted to protect workers from unsafe conditions and provide insurance benefits. The Roanoke workers, who are the subject of this book, belonged to the Brotherhood of Railway and Airline Clerks (BRAC). Their experiences are interesting because some were already working for the railroad before the racial changes that occurred nationally during the 1960s. Some of them briefly remarked on joining the union and their perceptions of membership. Not surprisingly, their job orientation seldom provided information about the union. Several respondents suggested that the need for joining the union and the subject of dues were matters that they later learned about sometime after beginning work for N&W. Some respondents did not mention the union

---

7. Eric Arnesen, "'Like Banquo's Ghost, It Will Not Down': The Race Question and the American Railroad Brotherhoods, 1880–1920," in *American Historical Review* 99.5 (December 1994), 1,608.

8. Arnesen, "'Like Banquo's Ghost,'" 1,608–09.

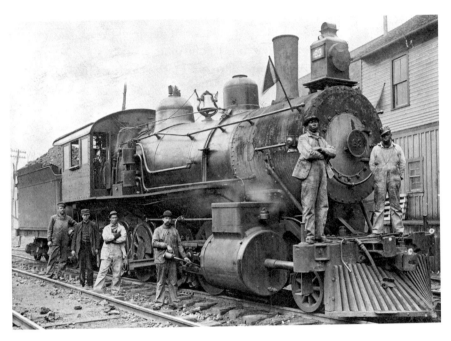

Class B steam engine No. 63 with its crew. *Norfolk Southern Corporation.*

at all, while others were vague about its necessity or functions. The two most eloquent responses about union membership came from John Mease, who spoke about the Norfolk & Western strike of 1978, and Mike Worrell, who serves as president of Division 301 of the Brotherhood of Locomotive Engineers and Trainmen. As an African American engineer whose father was an active union member, he asserts that "the unions gave a lot of people weekend pay, weekends off, set work schedules and [provided] good, safe work environments…and today we try to still follow that." For Worrell, unions facilitate safe working conditions and protect the rights of employees.

The pool of respondents for this project is small—there are only twenty. Even though the scope of the project may seem insignificant, it is not. It provides pieces for a much larger mosaic of railroad history and African American history. The stories that the respondents tell attest to the remarkable changes in the railroad industry and African American history. That history marks extraordinary progress for black workers who began only as construction workers who built the tracks to engineers. Additionally, there is a nostalgic side. The era when Norfolk & Western had a thriving passenger train business is long gone. No longer can small boys await one of its passenger trains in Buena Vista, Virginia, or other small towns. Fortunately, the chronicles contained in this book contribute to the ongoing story of American people and American railroads. This project also contributes to the history of Roanoke.

Theodore Carter DeLaney, PhD
Associate Professor of History
Director of Africana Studies
Washington and Lee University
Lexington, Virginia
March 24, 2014

ACKNOWLEDGEMENTS

This book would not have been possible without a number of individuals and organizations. First, I am grateful to all of my interviewees for generously sharing their stories with me. I'd also like to thank the members of the Norfolk & Western African American Heritage Group, especially its president and "spiritual leader" Al Holland.

I very much appreciate the Historical Society of Western Virginia for giving me the opportunity to conduct the oral history project and compile this book. I specifically would like to thank former executive director Jeanne M. Bollendorf; current chairs of the Kegley Publication Committee, George Kegley and Nelson Harris; and Registrar Linda Steele. I am also indebted to Norfolk Southern (NS) and to Jennifer D. McDaid, NS historical archivist, who tirelessly helped me track down many of the photographs, captions and other factual material. The Virginia Museum of Transportation and its excellent staff, including Executive Director Beverly T. Fitzpatrick Jr., Fran Ferguson, Peg McGuire and especially Curator and Historian Deena B. Sasser contributed much to this volume.

The oral history project was sponsored by the Virginia Foundation for the Humanities. I thank that group for its support. Pearl Transcripts did an excellent job of transcribing the many and varied transcripts. I am very grateful to Art Sellers of the Roanoke Camera Club for taking the beautiful photographs of the interviewees. This book is much improved by the essays contributed by local scholars and experts Dr. Theodore Carter DeLaney, Dr. C.W. Sullivan III and George Kegley. In addition, I thank my friend and colleague Dr. Martha Norkunas, professor at Middle Tennessee State University, who read a draft of my introductory essay and gave me valuable comments.

Finally, I would like to thank my husband, Chip, for bringing me to this enchanted land along the Blue Ridge Mountains, for his constant encouragement and support and for being "chief cook and bottle washer" while I was working on this project and manuscript. I'm grateful to my son Benjamin, who was writing his PhD dissertation on the West Coast while I was writing this book on the East Coast. We have always been simpatico. The stories I heard from these African American railroaders—those of education, family values, dedication and love—rang true.

INTRODUCTION

Roanoke is one of America's great rail centers and prides itself on that history; it was the original headquarters to N&W Railway for one hundred years and continues to be an important location for Norfolk Southern Corporation, the result of the 1982 merger of N&W and Southern Railways. As Dr. Theodore Carter DeLaney points out in his essay, African Americans have a long history with the railroad—a history that began before the Civil War, when enslaved people helped construct tracks across the country, and exists through to the present day. African Americans have played important roles in the history of the N&W Railway, as well as the Norfolk Southern. Those roles have evolved over time as laws have changed and doors of opportunity have opened. This book endeavors to tell the stories of some of these railroaders "in their own words," whose careers spanned the years from Jim Crow to the civil rights movement to today's institutional diversity programs. Some of the stories are the stories of pioneers who paved the way to today's more level playing field, and some are the stories of their children and grandchildren who have become engineers, conductors and corporate managers, positions that were denied to earlier generations. And in many cases, in telling their own stories, they tell the stories of their fathers or grandfathers who worked for the railroad and their mothers or grandmothers who urged them on and supported them. It is a multi-generational tapestry of voices that tells the story of struggle, resilience and triumph. This book is the result of interviews with some of the individuals who worked on the railroad. I conducted interviews in 2013 with retired Norfolk & Western and

Class R switching steam engine No. 397 with swallowtail tank, built September 1893. *Norfolk Southern Corporation.*

Norfolk Southern railroad employees, as well as those who are currently employed by Norfolk Southern in the Roanoke Valley.

African American Heritage on the Norfolk & Western, 1930–1970

Although the oral history project and book came into being rather quickly—over the course of two years—the idea for the book had been in the works for a long time. In 1998, an oral history project was developed by the Virginia Museum of Transportation (VMT). The purpose was to help create an exhibit focusing on African American railroaders. This exhibit is now a permanent installation, "African American Heritage on the Norfolk & Western, 1930–1970," and includes photographs, artifacts and a compelling video montage of railroaders telling their stories. There were twenty short interviews conducted between 1998 and 2000 by several volunteer interviewers, and eleven stories are featured in the video. The individuals featured in the video are: Lee Graves, John Divers, George E. Rogers, William C. Johnson, Sylvester G. Ford, Al Holland, George R. Long, Carroll Swain, Clinton Scott, Carl Tinsley and James W. Burks Jr. There are many interesting stories and experiences shared in the video, but I want to single out James W. Burks Jr.'s comments. Mr. Burks, who died in 2009, was one of the first African Americans in the N&W's management training program and in management. He was employed by the railroad from 1966 to 1998 and worked in a variety of departments, including computer services, management information, finance and coal marketing. As was the case with many of the individuals I interviewed, being one of the first to break a color barrier, Mr. Burks was highly conscious of his role. He remembers, "During the training program, I had an experience with the chief engineer, whose name I can't recall. One of his questions to me was what I thought I could do for the railroad. I told him I was there to show people that African Americans could do things other than sweep floors and build track. That was my main objective for coming here, although I did plan to get paid while I was doing it."

N&W AFRICAN AMERICAN HERITAGE GROUP

The development of the installation at VMT has its own interesting history. In Carroll Swain's interview, he details how the exhibit came about. In the 1990s, former VMT director Kay Strickland asked the Roanoke City Council for funding for an exhibit about the railroad. Mr. Swain was a council member at the time, and he remembers what he told her: "I can't vote for this because you're asking for something, and I don't see the contributions of African Americans to the railroad." Thus began a conversation, a walk through the museum and the suggestion for the exhibit, now the installation "African American Heritage on the Norfolk & Western, 1930–1970," which details those contributions. Another positive result of the conversation begun on behalf of African American railroad history is that a group of retirees began meeting at the museum once a month. Now in its nineteenth year, the group still meets and has a yearly celebration at the museum and provides an annual scholarship to a minority student at Virginia Western Community College. The group has

Members of the N&W African American Heritage Group, 2014. *Photo by Art Sellers.*

close ties with VMT and current executive director Beverly T. Fitzpatrick Jr. because, in addition to the installation, the museum has supported their efforts, monthly meetings and yearly celebrations over these many years. The group has expanded and is now joined by current Norfolk Southern employees. This younger group has taken it upon itself to give back to the community by forming two groups for young people—Rails of Color and CABOOSE, which are mentoring and afterschool programs in Roanoke. Norfolk Southern historical archivist Jennifer D. McDaid is a member of Rails of Color and attends the meetings as well. Many of the interviewees for the current oral history project came from this group.

COTTON TO SILK: ORAL HISTORIES OF AFRICAN AMERICAN WORKERS ON THE NORFOLK & WESTERN RAILROAD

The Historical Society of Western Virginia (HSWV), in partnership with the VMT, approached me in 2012 about the possibility of doing this oral history project. In part, the extension of the earlier project and the participation of the HSWV were due to Al Holland and George Kegley's long friendship. Kegley, a former longtime *Roanoke Times* business editor, director emeritus of the historical society and current co-chair of the society's Kegley Publications Committee, shares some of his thoughts about this project in his essay included in this book. Our first order of business was to write a grant to the Virginia Foundation for the Humanities, and we were lucky enough to receive funds. I began to conduct historical background research and prepare for the interviews.

The oral history project is called "Cotton to Silk: Oral Histories of African American Workers on the Norfolk & Western." The title of the project was taken from a quotation from one of the project's key participants, Al Holland. In 1998, he said, "We made cotton, but we took that cotton and made silk." What he meant was that when he was hired by the railroad in 1938, there were only certain jobs available to African Americans. These jobs were cleaners, crewmen, brakemen, porters, cooks and waiters. They were low-paying jobs compared with other railroad positions available only to white employees. Mr. Holland remembers that the railroaders "took what we could get" and made lives for themselves and their families. They bought homes, sent their children to school and were leaders in their communities. Eventually, after passage of the Civil Rights Act in 1964, they were able to bid on other jobs in the company and move up in the hierarchy to become clerks, machinists, supervisors, conductors, engineers and even vice-presidents.

I conducted twenty interviews for the project. One of the project's goals was to expand the information gathered by the VMT oral history project fifteen years ago. I re-interviewed the seven narrators from the earlier project who were still living: Al Holland, John Divers, Lee Graves, J.R. Hughes, Clinton Scott, Carroll Swain and Carl Tinsley. In addition to conducting longer and more in-depth interviews with these seven men, I also sought to diversify the stories. I included younger employees who hold positions that were opened up in the 1960s and '70s, as well as more women. The interviewees range in age from forty to ninety-eight. They also held or had held a variety of positions, including janitor, clerk, machinist, police officer, fireman, track laborer, brakeman, cook, engineer, conductor and vice-president. The interviewees worked for the railroad anywhere from two to forty-seven years. For a variety of reasons, I was only able to add one woman's story.

I recorded thirty hours of interviews between February and July 2013. Those interviews were transcribed, edited, returned to interviewees for approval and edited again. There were close to one thousand pages of interview transcripts. The approved, edited interview transcripts and digital recordings will be housed in the archives of the HMWV, and a virtual exhibit will be produced and will reside on the museum's website. Copies of the transcripts will also be housed in the Norfolk Southern Archives and the VMT. Material from the interviews will be used to update and expand the installation at the VMT.

African American Railroad Workers of Roanoke: Oral Histories of the Norfolk and Western

Once we had a publisher, deadline and limited word count for the manuscript, decisions had to be made about which interview excerpts to include. This was very difficult—possibly the most difficult of all the processes involved with the project. Decisions were made based on the stories' poignancy, power and thematic importance. Powerful themes emerged from the interviews—themes concerning a thriving African American community in Roanoke that, in some ways, no longer exists; the strong role the railroad and the black "railroad man" played within this community; the importance of mentors, black and white; the power of education; commitment and a strong work ethic; and the importance of self-respect, quiet strength, determination and giving back to the larger community. These tight bonds of kinship and community are explored more fully in Dr. C.W. Sullivan's essay. Suffice it to say here that most of the interviewees were raised in families with fathers, uncles, grandfathers, other family members or "father figures" who worked for Norfolk & Western, and today many of them also have siblings and children who work for Norfolk Southern.

As one might imagine, with bridging the time period between Jim Crow and today, there are quite a few "firsts" in this group of interviewees. For the N&W Roanoke Division, there was the first African American machinist, clerk in Freight Traffic, supervisor of the East End Shops, police officer and engineer. For the Virginia Division, there was the first chief dispatcher and the first operational vice-president not only for N&W but for the entire railroad industry. There is a profound awareness that the people who came before made their positions possible. This is so ably said by David Cobbs:

N&W signal repairmen, 1929. *Norfolk Southern Corporation.*

"The Al Hollands of the world…blazed the trail. They put up with stuff that probably I wouldn't have been able to put up with. By the time I got out here, for the most part, it was accepted that if you were black, you could make it out here. I think that's why I've been successful, why Terry Evans has been successful and why any number of African Americans out there have been successful. They [made] the way better for me."

The narrators discuss some of their experiences with racism and discrimination. But for the most part, the major story they wanted to tell me was one of triumph over that racism. In the older generation, the self-styled "Cottons," the ones who experienced the Jim Crow years and were prevented from moving up in the company, triumphed by providing for their families and, in most cases, moving on to higher positions after the Civil Rights Act. The generation that was hired after the Civil Rights Acts, the "Silks"—especially those with college educations—triumphed by being hired as management trainees and staying the course by confronting racist situations directly or going through the proper corporate channels. Even one of the younger interviewees encountered some racist attitudes from co-workers (not the corporation) that were "underground," but those were dealt with and didn't impair his career or enjoyment of his work.

The truth is, even after 1964, Norfolk & Western was slow to change. But today, Norfolk Southern has a strong, award-winning diversity initiative and has an assistant vice-president of EEO and Diversity who happens to be African American and heads a large staff that is dedicated to diversifying the company not only with regard to race but also with regard to gender, geographic background and thinking style, to name a few. One of my interviewees, Terry Evans, the first African American vice-president of Transportation, spoke in his interview about how the railroad has changed as America has changed and will evolve even more in the future: "The railroad is a byproduct of America. [There is] no way for the railroad not to become more diverse when the employee base is becoming more diverse. It's just a natural progression of things...You take a snapshot of America, and you could almost take that same number in the snapshot, and that's the railroad. We go to the same hiring base as everyone else in America, and as America changes—and the country is changing—that will be our workforce." Mr. Swain, one of the older interviewees, noted that still more needs to be done: "I appreciate what I see out there now, but things are still not where they should be, not even with Norfolk Southern. It's not where it should be, but they're working on it."

In the chapters that follow, the narrators speak for themselves. In order to have more room for the stories and increase their impact, I've removed my questions from the interview excerpts. The full transcripts will be available at the HMWV archives. The interviews were open-ended, but my questions included subjects such as childhood background; education; mentors; recreation; other railroaders in the family; milestones of career/positions held; segregation; instances of racism; union activities; duties and responsibilities of their positions; the effects of Jim Crow, World War II and the Civil Rights Act on their working life; and the impact that working for the railroad has had on their children and grandchildren. The interview excerpts were edited for accuracy and readability, while preserving the narrators' meanings.

The book is greatly improved by having the essays of three local experts in the fields of African American history, occupational folklore and the Roanoke Valley included. Dr. DeLaney's essay speaks to the railroad history of African Americans that is the backdrop of this project and details the difficult conditions and enormous gains that have been made by

A group of employees at the Bluefield, West Virginia yard, June 1929. *Norfolk Southern Corporation.*

African American railroaders over the course of the twentieth century. Dr. Sullivan's essay elaborates on the themes of kinship and community that are such a strong aspect of the stories told in this volume, especially the roles of fathers and grandfathers who were the respected "railroad men." George Kegley's essay offers insight into how the railroad influenced the local community, his friendship with Al Holland and why the HSWV took such an interest in seeing this oral history project and book to completion. Their essays, as well as this one, will be part of the virtual exhibit on the HMWV website.

Finally, a word about oral history. As Dr. DeLaney points out, oral history is the remembrances of individuals "as they remember it" and as such portrays the nuances of past experiences and memories without necessarily adhering to strict chronologies and historical detail. As editor, I take complete responsibility for any dates and facts that are incorrect, names misspelled or other inaccuracies. Every effort has been made to ensure the material is free from error.

Due to space limitations, not all of the interviewees' stories were included in this book. I wish excerpts could have been included from all the interviews, as each one has a particular power, beauty and truth. The expanded, updated exhibit at VMT, the virtual exhibit and the archived interviews at HMWV exist as partners with this book in telling these stories more completely, as the story is ongoing, complicated and complex.

Although there have been recent publications that address the role African Americans have played in the building and maintaining of America's railroads, none has focused on the Roanoke Valley or the Norfolk & Western Railway. It is my hope that this book will help document the lives and careers of African Americans living and working in Southwestern Virginia in one of the most American of industries—the railroad—and through some of the most tumultuous and momentous events of the twentieth century. I feel honored to have been a part of this project and hope that the publication of the book, an updated exhibit at the VMT, an online exhibit and the archiving of these interviews will encourage others to continue the work of documenting the contributions of African American railroad workers in the Roanoke area. Finally, I hope the book lives up to Mike Worrell's sentiment about publishing these stories: "That's a good thing because everybody needs to hear it. Not only is it a story of them, it's actually a story of the railroad or how the railroad got to where they are at. Without those stories, there wouldn't be an America." As David Cobbs told the *Roanoke Times* (February 16, 2014), "This is not just African American history, this is everybody's story."

Sheree Scarborough

The Stories

Chapter 1

AL HOLLAND

Al Holland, 2013. *Photo by Art Sellers.*

Alphonzo L. Holland was born in 1916 in Roanoke. He attended the historically black Hampton Institute, now Hampton University, but did not graduate. He returned to Roanoke, got married and began working for Norfolk & Western in 1938. He hired on as a janitor, the only job he could get at the time. His father, Gus Holland, worked for N&W as a laborer and blacksmith, and his brother Theodore Holland also worked for N&W. Mr. Holland served in the army during World War II in the Philippines. He worked for N&W as a janitor, freight handler, watchman and head clerk. He retired in 1985 as assistant manager in Tariff Compilations. He served forty-six years with the railroad. In addition, Mr. Holland was a member of the Roanoke Cardinals, a semipro baseball team; a member of the Twilight Singers, a singing group of the N&W Freight Station; a Boy Scout leader for fifty years at High Street Baptist Church; and president of the Roanoke chapter of the NAACP in the late 1960s and early '70s, among other community affiliations. Mr. Holland was named Roanoke Citizen of the Year in 2003 and is a founding member of the N&W African American Heritage Group.

My Father Was a Blacksmith on the N&W

"Norfolk & Western made this town."

I was the fourth child in my family, and my father, Gus Holland, was on the railroad then, where he stayed. When I realized what he was doing, he was a blacksmith. I guess I was around seven or eight years old then, and I could see him coming home with his lunch bucket. He walked to work. He never bought an automobile. I never lived in a rented house because he bought the house we lived in and walked to work every day. When they found out he was skillful, they made him a blacksmith. I can't say how much money he was making at that time. You see, Norfolk & Western made this town. If you could get a job on the Norfolk & Western at that time, you were home free. My daddy went from laborer to blacksmith, and when you go down there again to the Virginia Museum of Transportation, look at that glass case. There's a hammer in there. My daddy made that for my eldest brother in 1908.

I was born in 1916. The next boy was born in 1919, and then there were ten of us altogether. We lived on what my daddy made, and we lived on Eighth Avenue Northwest. My mother—at that time, there weren't any washing machines—brought us up on washing boards. We had chickens in the backyard, and we never went hungry because we could raise chickens and get eggs. Daddy had a lot on the other side, two doors up the street, that he plowed every summer [to grow] cabbage, beans, squash, tomatoes and cucumbers. He put all that in that lot, and all we didn't use, Mama canned. When it got cold, she always had that food back in that closet there. She just opened up a can of string beans or a can of soup. There were half-gallon jugs. Nobody was ever hungry.

At that time, we had stoves in every room. You could get coal for six dollars a ton. With my father being on the railroad, when they'd take those crossties out, he'd get those crossties and bring them home. He'd get somebody to haul them home with a wagon. He had a crosscut saw and cut those crossties into stove length, split them open. They had a lot of wooden boxcars then. When they scrapped boxcars, he'd get wood for kindling. We'd have to cut that kindling—put it on the back porch and then cut that wood up. We brought the coal up from the coalhouse down on the alley and brought it up on the back porch.

I'll never forget one time when my brother James and I were out there doing something. I remember it was on a Wednesday because my daddy went to prayer meeting—and we didn't cut any kindling—so he came in from the prayer meeting. He went upstairs, and we were in the bed. He went in there and looked at that wood box out on the back porch. "Alphonzo?" "Yes, Papa?" I said. "I don't see any wood in that wood box." "Well, I was going to cut it in the morning," I said. "Oh, you're not going to cut it in the morning. You're going to get up and cut it now. And don't turn that light on the back porch—you cut that wood." I didn't let that happen anymore.

We walked to school. We walked to church. The church then was old High Street Baptist Church. My father made sure that we got our shoes ready on Saturday and got there on Sunday morning by walking to the old High Street Baptist Church for Sunday school. He was a stickler for time. He was a great man, and I really appreciated him. He's been dead now about thirty-something years. And as I said, he was a blacksmith for the railroad. They had a building and built drive shafts for the engines. Anything that had to be made, the blacksmith had to make it—drive shafts and wheels and so forth.

N&W STARS

"If you could play baseball, Roy Gable would hire you."

There was a baseball team, the N&W Stars. If you could play baseball, Roy Gable would hire you. And he didn't put them in harm's way where they'd be lifting anything. He had them wiping down engines and so forth. Those were his children because he loved his baseball, and he was the superintendent at the Sixteenth Street Roundhouse. He'd follow those baseball players anywhere. If they were playing anywhere, he was gone. My daddy was the blacksmith at Sixteenth Street [Roundhouse] at that time.

And when they had picnics, they'd have excursions. They'd run an excursion train to some particular base for the whites and come right back and run one for the coloreds. I was a little boy running around at that time. We had our excursion to Pulaski. Mom packed the basket, and we got on the train from Roanoke to Pulaski. If they would run the excursion for the whites, they would run one for the Negroes. We went up to Pulaski, and that ball club…they'd probably go up there and play ball on the field while we were up there. We'd have a good time. In the picture I donated to the museum, you can see a boy sitting down beside the team. Lee Calloway was the manager, and that was

The N&W Stars baseball team worked under the supervision of Roy Gable, superintendent of the N&W Sixteenth Street Roundhouse. Team members who can be identified include Jim Jones (#2), Bob Jefferson (#3), Jess Smith (#4), "Bubba" McAfee (#5), Early Edwards (#6), "Botley" Colston (#7), Manager Lee Calloway (#8), Jack Calloway (#9) and Tom Payne (#13). *Virginia Museum of Transportation.*

Lee Calloway's son. You'll see that picture sitting on the wall if you go down there and look for it. His name was Jack. He and I went to school together in grade school. We'd go over at Springwood Park and chase balls for them. We were paid fifteen or twenty cents. I was too young to play for the N&W Stars, but later I played for the Roanoke Cardinals, a black semipro baseball team.

N&W WAS THE BEST JOB I COULD GET

"We made cotton, but we took that cotton and made silk."

I went to work for Norfolk & Western in 1938. It was the best job I could get because the steel mill wasn't paying as much as the railroad was. There

Package cars at the Roanoke Freight Station, March 1936. *Norfolk Southern Corporation.*

wasn't any other outfit paying as much as the railroad for labor, and that's what I would be getting, a laboring job. I went with the railroad. The first job I had was cleaning in the General Office Building. At that time, there was a cuspidor at every desk. I had to clean those cuspidors and make sure the desk and everything was clean. It was an unthinkable situation, but of course we had gloves we could use. I needed the job. My kids needed the food, so I had to work somewhere.

I stayed with the railroad, and I went to work at the Freight Station for a few years. I think it was in 1941–42 that I worked at the Freight Station.

Then, in 1943, I was called to the military. I had two children then. They were drafting people aged eighteen to forty-five, and I was in that category, so I had to go. I left here on the twenty-third day of February to go to New Cumberland, Pennsylvania. It was a cold, good morning up there when we got our outfits. We had to stay inside because it was too cold to go outside. So I came down, and I went to Fort Belvoir with this outfit of combat engineers. I was with the Thirty-eighth Division and served in the Philippines. I was a corporal, but when I came out, I was a sergeant first class. We were in a segregated army. It was segregated all the way through.

I was hired as a janitor but moved up to the Freight Station. I was a freight handler because when they hit Pearl Harbor, more jobs opened up. But then they continued the draft, and they got me in the draft in 1943. I had to leave the Freight Station. If we got back, our job was supposed to be there for us, which it was. When I came back in 1946, I went back to the Freight Station. That's when I built a house on $0.62 an hour. Eugene Brown was the contractor, and he built that house for me that's standing today on Staunton Avenue, a cinder-block stucco, for $9,500.00. My notes were $40.00 a month. I walked to work. I hadn't bought a car yet because I couldn't afford a house and a car at the same time.

That's why I'm saying "from cotton to silk." We took what we could get, and we made a life for ourselves. Our children went to school. You can't say we took the money and squandered it. We made cotton, but we took that cotton and made silk. We've got men coming down meeting with us for the Heritage Group at the Transportation Museum, and they're engineers, conductors, firemen—those jobs are open to them. We had to take what we had down here because we weren't going to get those jobs. But I lived to see them get it. They didn't have to come in and clean cuspidors; they went through training and got hired as engineers and got to move on to conductors.

TWILIGHT SINGERS

"We were different from the N&W singers; we were strictly from the Freight Station."

When I was at the Freight Station, I was involved with the Twilight Singers. A fellow by the name of Ira Womack, who was very gifted at singing, started working and singing with us. And so we started singing. We sang gospel

The N&W Male Chorus performing at Roanoke's Academy of Music. *Virginia Museum of Transportation.*

music. We had about fifteen men. I was the lead singer. We went to churches and to the YMCA. We raised money for the YMCA, and we'd sing a lot of times down there for things happening at the Freight Station. We were different from the N&W singers; we were strictly from the Freight Station. The N&W singers were sponsored by the company, which bought their tuxedo uniforms for them. But we bought our own—black suits. We didn't have any competition, but sometimes we'd sing on the same program.

I STARTED MOVING UP

"When I retired, I was the assistant manager in Tariff Compilations."

So then I started moving up. We got more movement and transportation. Before we were trucking with two wheels, but then we got motorized, moving the freight up and down the platform from car to car. I had to go down to the Passenger Station and load the mail on the passenger train because they were cutting out the freight. They were closing down the Freight House, so I went to the Passenger Station on the passenger train and was loading mail on the passenger train when it come through. Then I got moved out of that, and I had to go back to the janitor position. There were men that were still working at the Freight Station who had more seniority than I did. So they pulled me out of there. And when you lose your job, they would have to find you another job. I went back to the General Office Building and the janitors, but all the cuspidors were gone then. But they had moved up from the $0.38. It was higher; it was at $1.75 an hour.

Then they needed security, so I was able to bid on security. It was a high-paying job. Segregation was going out with the passage of the Civil Rights Act, and you could bid. I had enough seniority, so I started bidding on the clerk jobs. I stayed in that clerk position until it opened up a little more. Al Mayer was the chief clerk. He was the one who was in charge of pricing and marketing. I was in the mailroom then, and so when we had what you call the freight cars, the ones hauling all the wheat, they had to be in a special car; it had to be a special time. I would go over and run the mimeograph machine with the letterhead so they could send the letters out on how they were going to move these wheat cars. I'd make about seven, eight copies of them.

Al came in one day and said, "Look, I know we just sent out some, but we've got some more cars to go out." I said, "Well, I've got it." He said, "You've got letters here for it?" I said, "Oh, yes, letters are here for it." I always made more than just one or two. So when the job came available for clerk, he said, "It's a good job, Holland, you can bid on it." It came through, and I had the job. I think it was the second clerk in pricing and marketing. So we moved down where the old Passenger Station was. I got a head clerk position there. I did that job.

When I was in the reserves, I had to go back to summer camp each summer. So I had to go down to summer camp for two weeks. One Sunday morning, I was at home and the telephone rang. Al called me up and said, "Al, I'm glad you're back." I said, "Well, thank you." He said, "Well, what are you doing?" I said, "I'm getting ready to go to church." He said, "Can you come down here for a minute?" I said, "Well, I'm going to church." He said, "Well, you don't have to stay that long. While you were gone, we decided that you needed to be the assistant chief clerk." I was on salary then. So I worked there for about two years straight, and then I kept moving up. When I retired, I was the assistant manager in Tariff Compilations.

When I was president of the NAACP, the vice-president of Personnel called me and said, "Mr. Holland, I know you're in the NAACP now, and I know we've got some diehards on this railroad." He said, "If you need any help of any kind, you come here to me." I had one encounter at that time, involving Curtis Hairston. He was on train service but wanted to be an engineer, and they wouldn't put him into service. He called me, and I said, "Well, let me see what we can do." So I went and talked to Mr. Parson, vice-president of Personnel. He said, "He's mighty young." I said, "Yes." He called Hairston's boss and asked him, "Has he put down that he wanted to be an engineer?" He said, "Yes, he put it down." He said to Hairston's boss, "Well, why didn't you put him in?" The boss said, "Well, I thought by him being a brakeman that he was satisfied." Parson said, "You don't think. You put him in there as a trainee to go in as an engineer." So he got it. He turned out to be one of the best engineers they had. They said one time he was coming over Christiansburg Mountain and the brakes went out, and he put that train in reverse and backed it on down over that mountain.

Chapter 2

JOSEPH JOHNSON

Joseph Johnson, 2014. *Photo by Art Sellers.*

Joseph C. Johnson was born in Darlington Heights, Virginia, in 1920. He moved to Roanoke as a child when his father got a job with Norfolk & Western as a laborer at Shaffer's Crossing. Mr. Johnson started working for N&W in 1944, during World War II, in the Dining Car Department. He retired after a forty-year career. His career was mostly spent in the dining cars, including a period on the private car of N&W president Richard Dunlap.

MR. MENEFEE AND THE N&W

"Go down and see if you can't get that job on the railroad."

Pearl Harbor happened on December 7, 1941. When the war broke out, I was working as a busboy at the Hotel Roanoke. I wanted to become a waiter because I used to see the way those boys—the regular waiters—got the tips that they got, and I said to myself, "I want to be a waiter." But I didn't have the experience, so awhile after the war broke out, I told myself, "What am I hollering about the hotel for? Go down and see if you can't get that job on the railroad."

I went down and talked to the superintendent of the dining car on the Norfolk & Western Railroad. I still remember him. His name was Jed W. Menefee. I talked with Mr. Menefee, and he said, "Well, what are you doing now?" I said, "I'm a busboy at Hotel Roanoke." I didn't tell any lies. But anyhow, I told him, "I work at Hotel Roanoke, and I'm a busboy." That's what I told Mr. Menefee on the railroad. He said, "Well, I'll tell you what you do. You go back up to the hotel, learn how to wait tables and then come back and talk to me," which I did. But I didn't take forever to get back to him. I went back right fast. The second or third time I went back, I didn't have any trouble getting the job—I think because the Japs had attacked us. He put me on, and I heard him say, "Mr. Thornton, sign this man up. We're going to send him as far as Bristol tomorrow. We're going to make a waiter out of him."

So he put me on the train that runs from New York to New Orleans, but Norfolk & Western didn't do all of that. Norfolk & Western worked that train from a place called Monroe, Virginia. That's where the Norfolk & Western took over this Southern [Railway] train. It went on down to Lynchburg and on up to Roanoke, where we got on it. And from Roanoke, Virginia, to Birmingham, Alabama, was my run. Now, the conductors, trainmen and all the rest of those guys who worked on that train would get off. Norfolk & Western men got off at Bristol. Some Southern men worked on down to Knoxville; when they got to Knoxville, that's as far south as they went. But the cooks and the waiters on those dining cars were all Norfolk & Western, so everybody else changed except Norfolk & Western men.

When we got on here at Roanoke, we went all the way to Birmingham, Alabama. And after we got down there, there wasn't anything to do. But everybody had heard about Alabama way back then and how they treated black people, so when we got to Birmingham, we didn't do a thing but get

Dining car with waiters and steward. *Virginia Museum of Transportation.*

off that train and go up to a lady's house where the company had hired this woman to sleep us overnight. We just went on up to her house and went to bed. The next morning, we got up, put our clothes on, came on down and climbed up on that diner and got ready to serve breakfast out of Birmingham. When breakfast was over, we got ourselves ready for lunch. Coming this way, we started serving lunch after we left Chattanooga, and that lunch would usually bring us all the way down here.

But eventually lunch was over. Then we'd get a chance to have something to eat for ourselves. And since no whites were being served, we'd get a chance to sit down and have our own meals and look out the window. Then it wasn't too long after we left Knoxville that we started getting ourselves ready for dinner that night. Coming this way, the train goes all the way to New York, but we got off at Roanoke and started getting ourselves ready for the evening meal. Anyhow, we always did have a pretty good meal on that train. Then, let's see, everything was over by the time we got in somewhere around those little stops up there between Bristol and Roanoke.

When we got to Roanoke, a yard engine would come and take our diner out of there and push it to one side. And that diner went right on back the next day. So that's the way it was. We'd make a trip down to Birmingham, and then when that trip was over, we'd come back. I think we had about a day or maybe two days at home, so those who had wives got to be with them. On the third day, we had to stock. When I say stock, that means putting food on the train because it's going out the next morning. You knew what to order, and you filled up your icebox with perishable stuff like chicken and steaks. And you also put fruit in there. These diners were kind of old. You'd have to put ice on top of them to keep your stuff [cold]. We didn't have this electric refrigeration like they have now. You'd go down there and see men take great big lumps of ice, and two or three of them would get this ice on top of this thing and push it down in there. That's how they kept the food.

For a while, I was in the service myself. I was stationed at Great Lakes, Illinois. I wrote Mr. Menefee a letter. I said, "Mr. Menefee, if you can send me a pass, that'll be my transportation between Roanoke and Great Lakes, Illinois." He said, "Joe Johnson, I would like to help you, but let me tell you something. I can't send you a pass every time you are getting ready to come home. I can't do that. I'll tell you what I will do. If you can find some kind of way to pay your way from Great Lakes, Illinois, to Cincinnati, then I'll have a pass for you from Cincinnati and back to Cincinnati. I'll do that for you." But in the service, things changed so fast. Before I could work out something about that, they had moved me out of Great Lakes and sent me down to Bainbridge, Maryland. Then, after I left Bainbridge, Maryland, I ended up in Florida.

SEGREGATED CARS

"They had curtains in the dining car."

They had curtains in the dining car. You could pull them by strings, and that would block you out from anybody else. The rest of the people on the train couldn't see you. But you still had to pay the same thing for your meal as the guy who wasn't being blotted out. Those cars were made to serve about thirty people. So a four-seat table right here got blocked out, and over on this side, there's four seats. And right across the little aisles, there's a table

Chef on dining car. *Norfolk Southern Corporation.*

that served two. You pull the curtain here for these four and pull that curtain for these two. That's how that went. When people came back to the diner and saw those curtains back there, they knew what was what, so they just turned around and went on back. Then, after a while, when business started slacking up a little bit and people were being fed, nobody stood around like they wanted to get a table. It wasn't too bad.

But I wasn't on the diner for forty years. As time went on, I was always searching for something that might be a little better. Have you ever heard the name [Richard Freeman] Dunlap? He was one of the presidents. He had his own private car. I worked for Mr. Dunlap. But he wasn't out there on that great, big, fine car by himself. He had his own room right here, but maybe the next two or three rooms down the hall were for other men. But it was your job to look after the man that you were assigned to. So I had Mr. Dunlap, and his little bed took up about as much space as half of this room. His bed was there, and there was also a place to wash up. That was for him. [It was] nice. We had a place. This is the kitchen. There's a place to cook, and when you come out of the kitchen, there's a place to seat eight or ten

42

people. It's not like a diner; this is a smaller place. I think the diner can be opened up to seat about ten or twelve people because there were times when we had we had to take care of certain parties.

Sometimes we'd serve [Mr. Dunlap] steak, and sometimes he'd have a roast chicken—whatever you can think of that's kind of fancy. There was always a special way to fix vegetables. And you'd have special bread. All we would need to do is take that bread and put it in the oven and get it warm. And wine—or if you wanted something else to drink—was also available.

There were some trains I worked on where you weren't supposed to eat the stuff that the big shots ate. You weren't supposed to have it. Of course, they weren't going to fire you, but they'd let you know that you were doing wrong. And the guys knew that they weren't supposed to have it, so they didn't bother it. All I wanted was something to eat. It didn't have to be anything special. But I was standing up there some mornings and looking at that Smithfield ham. There's no ham in the world like Smithfield ham, but they didn't want the help to have the ham. The superintendent would come around sometimes, and he'd tell the chef, "Chef, the way this ham has been cut here, I'll tell you what you can do. Give the hock ends to the help. You know we're not going to serve a hock end to somebody paying all that money to ride the train. They're going to have a center cut of Smithfield. That's what kind of ham they're going to have." But that was all right. The hock end just tastes so good.

Before I retired, I worked in the Motive Power Building and was a messenger; I delivered mail. But anytime Mr. Dunlap wanted to go somewhere, they'd send a message down to the Motive Power Building: "We need Joe Johnson up here." So I'd go up there and find out where they were going and when they wanted me down here. That's the way it went, and nobody better tell them that they can't get Joe Johnson.

Chapter 3

CLINTON SCOTT

Clinton Scott, 2013. *Photo by Art Sellers.*

Clinton D. Scott was born in Roanoke in 1921. Mr. Scott attended Lucy Addison High School but left before graduation when he was in the eleventh grade. He started working for Norfolk & Western in 1941, when he was twenty years old. His father, George Scott, worked for N&W for thirty-seven years as a janitor. His brother, George Scott Jr., also worked for N&W as a janitor. Mr. Scott worked in a variety of positions, including at the scrap wharf for the Yard Department, as wheel roller for the Wheel Department and in the Machine Shop, where he became a supervisor. He was the first African American supervisor in the East End Shops. Mr. Scott worked for the railroad for forty years, retiring in 1981.

Wheel Roller

"We sent for horses, and they sent ponies."

I started working [at Norfolk & Western] in November 1941. I went to the railroad when I was eighteen, and I was small. Mr. Black, a superintendent, worked at the Motive Power [Building] with my father, and he told me, "The day you hit twenty, you have a job." I turned twenty on the twenty-first, and I went to work on the twenty-sixth. It was a weekend. I got a job just like he promised me. My brother got hired, and my brother-in-law got hired. I got hired two days after my brother-in-law.

[My first job was at] the scrap wharf. [It was] in the Yard Department, but they called it a scrap wharf. Most of us were hired through the scrap wharf the first time because it was wartime, and they would distribute men from different places in the shop where they needed them. Whenever they needed them, they would send them from the scrap wharf. But most of them went to the scrap wharf and then to various parts of the shop.

[Pearl Harbor] affected everything because the railroad had iron railings to guard different places. They took the iron railings up and put down wooden railings because they needed all the metal that they could [get] so we could have supplies for the boys overseas. [My job was to] sort scrap. All kinds of metal was separated, and [then they would] sell it or ship it to different places. After that, they sent me to the Wheel Shop. I got a job rolling wheels for three cents more on labor. I was the smallest wheel roller. I was really sent over there as a joke. The Wheel Shop foreman and the yard foreman didn't get along. They wanted me in the Wheel Shop, but they wanted everybody in the Wheel Shop to weigh 200 pounds, and I weighed 136.

They sent two of us, and when we got over there, we were teased. They said, "We sent for horses, and they sent ponies." They said, "We wanted some men; we didn't want boys." I thought I was a pretty good man at twenty-one, twenty-two. So I was determined to learn how to roll wheels. After I learned how to roll wheels, one day the yard foreman was passing through the Wheel Shop, and the Wheel Shop foreman said, "Come in here. I'm going to show you them boys that you sent over here." He showed him me rolling the wheel. He got back at him.

It's mostly a sense of balance. A man told me that if I could ride a bicycle, I could roll a wheel. He was just about right. I learned a sense of balance on a wheel. You could actually take one of those 750-pound wheels and balance

Wheel rolling demonstration. *Norfolk Southern Corporation.*

it, and you can put your hands on it and hold it up. But you better know how to balance it.

I got injured [pretty soon after being hired] in 1942. That ankle right there is bigger, and then this one got crushed. A wheel fell on it from a boxcar. They used to send wheels there in boxcars, and they [would] generally be on an angle. This time, the front two—they had braces across—were on the angle, and we would roll them down a ramp. You had to put them in pairs. Some of them were 235s, 240s—they went in pairs. We took the railing out and started rolling them out, but during the travel from here and where they brought them, they straightened them up some. I went back to get the next one, and a man hollered and the whole roll fell down right across there. It just flattened out. They carried me to the doctor's office about halfway from the shop, and the ambulance took me there to the LewisGale [Hospital]. We had to go up in what we called "the attic." Up at the top of LewisGale, they had two or three beds for the colored, and they gave me some needles and some kind of tablet for pain. The foreman came up there while I was under that medicine and told me to sign something to show that there had been an accident down there. And I signed away the rights and that I was at fault in the accident. They didn't treat us like human beings. [It said that] I should have watched, that I should have done this and that and that it was my fault. We weren't in a union then.

About ten or eleven years after that, this foreman got fired. He got fired for drinking. He was an alcoholic, but he was a brilliant man in the Wheel Shop. He could just look at it and tell you how much to trim off. He knew his job, but he was an alcoholic and didn't have any sympathy for a black man. He cracked jokes about them all the time. [On] pretty days, we could work in-house, but as soon as you get the rain, he'd send us outdoors to do things in the rain. He was terrible.

The way I did it—and maybe it was wrong—but I stood up to him seriously one day. It sounds bad on both of our parts. I asked him to get off to go up to the Red Cross. I'd been in the service and come back, and they sent me a letter, the Red Cross, to come back and put in an application for injuries I'd gotten in the service. They had a checkup there for me also. I went up to the office to ask to go there. He was about half drunk [and said], "Take off that 'so-and-so' cap you got on for a hat." He said it in a terrible manner; I won't say what he said. I looked around the office and said, "I don't see a woman in here—why should I take my hat off for a man?" He said, "The rest of them boys down there do it." I said, "I'm not a boy, though." He told me to get the 'so-and-so' out of here and told the clerk, "Write him up and give him a pink slip."

I went on up to where my daddy was and told him what [happened]. So he went into the big office where the high officials [were], and he had a talk with them. Then the man told me to come in there. He said, "You go ahead and do your business, and then you go on back to work and lose some of that temper you've got. We're going to take care of that other one down there." I went on up to the Red Cross and came back, and he came to me [and said], "You up there running your big mouth with the white shirts?" I said, "No, but I want to tell you this: if you don't get out of my face, I'm going to cut you as long as I can catch up with you." I meant it, and from then on, we were friends. He was terrible, but he told me, "I believe you could." I said, "I got tired of all the jokes you told about the black woman and the boss going to his house. I got tired of that. In the service, we had all colors. We didn't have that kind of stuff in California." He said, "Well, I'm sorry. The rest of the boys seemed like they enjoyed it." I said, "Well, I didn't enjoy it."

Finally, I bid on another job up at the shop driving a truck. I drove the truck at the shop for a good while. When they said they were going to cut the laborers in about 1957—there were about three hundred and some, and they were going to cut all of them—we had to go up there and sign up where we were going and which way we wanted to go. When I got up to the clerk, he said, "C.D., I know where you are going." They had already assigned me back to the Wheel Shop. I said, "I was going to go into the freight line, but you all assigned me back to the Wheel Shop." He said, "Well, that don't make a difference, [I can change it]." I said, "No, I'll take it just like you've got it." So I went on back to the Wheel Shop. The foreman came to me and said they were going to cut off all of the laborers and keep seven. He said, "You'll be in the seven." I said, "How am I going to be in the seven when you've got a lot of men with more seniority than me?" I drove a truck and also rolled wheels, so he said, "Wheel roller and truck driver. If you can do both, then you can't [be pulled]." Most of them looked at those wheels, and so many people got hurt learning. [They said], "I don't want that. I don't want to get hurt. I'd rather get my unemployment for a while." I was in the seven that were left.

Mrs. Pevler's Garden

"I'm not going to promise you anything."

At first, before I got saved, I used to do a lot of different things, even on the job. But after I got saved and went to the church in 1956, the headman came through the shop. He was a lay preacher, and he was one of the best men. I said, "Mr. 'So-and-So,' I've joined the church." He said, "That's good," and he kept walking. About thirteen years later, the supervisor in there told me, "Go up to the shop." He asked me first. He came in there one evening and said, "How would you like to be a supervisor?" This was 1969. I said, "Over what? N&W don't have nothing for black men other than a helper." He said, "Well, don't say anything about it." It was that evening when we were getting ready to quit. The next morning, I got the truck because I used to go and pick up tools and different things and bring them back. He said, "Go up there and see the superintendent this morning." I said, "What do you want me to bring back—anything special?" He said, "No, don't take the truck, just walk up there." So I walked up there and said, "What's going on?"

I met the general foreman. I went to the clerk first to get permission to go see the foreman. I went in there and said, "Good morning, Mr. So-and-So."

He said, "I'm not going to promise you anything." I'm telling you just like he told me. Nobody had promised me anything to start with, so I didn't know what he was talking about. He said, "Go on over there and walk around with [Mr. So-and-So]. He's retiring. I've got a white boy on that job, and he's doing a good job. You just go in there and walk around with Mr. So-and-So." I went on out there and walked with him. He was going to retire at the end of that week. He walked around to different ones and told jokes and drank coffee. I just followed him along.

We had our safety meeting every morning, and come Monday, nobody said I had the job or anything. I just came down and got the time clock like I had been seeing him do, and we had our safety class for five minutes. I didn't know where any of the men worked. I said, "You all go do your various jobs, and you won't have no problem out of me if you stay on your job and do your job. We're going to get along very well." I sent them off to the job. Then I went around and found out what they were doing.

I was the labor supervisor or labor foreman, but nobody told me I was the supervisor. During that time, I had about twenty-five or thirty I supervised. They worked all over. I had to go around and find out what all of them were doing because I'd never been up there to do that kind of work. Somebody said that the government said [there] had to be somebody in the supervisor's position in different jobs. That's one of the reasons. I think the main reason I got the job was because of the general superintendent of the shop that was over this foreman. He came to me one day and said, "C.D., come on take a ride with me. I'm going to the president's house. Mrs. Pevler wants somebody to help her in her flower garden. I thought about you—this a good time you can witness. I heard they were big-timers, and you might give witness to them and get them to go to church."

He knocked on the door, and we went on in. [Mrs. Pevler] said, "You all come in. Would you like to have tea, lemonade or a soft drink, anything you all want to drink?" She had a little meal for us out there, and she said, "You know anything about gardening?" I said, "Natural garden I do, but flowers I don't know about. But I'm willing to learn." She said, "I want you to work every Saturday from seven to three o'clock." I said, "I cannot. I can work from seven to eleven. I drive the church bus. The little kindergarten children…I bring them to church every Saturday for their class." She asked, "You do that on your time?" I said, "Every Saturday, and I wouldn't like to break that circle." She said, "If you do that for the church, you and I are going to get along very well." It wasn't any time after that they made me supervisor. I don't know if that had anything to do with it or not, but I met the president, and he liked my work out there with her. She had a regular man, but he drank, and sometimes she couldn't find him on Saturdays. When he didn't show up, she'd call me, and I'd go out there. She specialized in azaleas. She was a millionaire, and you wouldn't know whether she was my sister or brother the way we talked. We talked about everything.

FIRST AFRICAN AMERICAN SUPERVISOR OF THE EAST END SHOPS

"Mr. Scott gives me all the nigger jobs."*

(*Editor's note: I have left the N-word in this excerpt because this is one of Mr. Scott's iconic stories, and it seems important to accurately convey the meaning of the story.)

I came from the Wheel Shop and went into the Machine Shop. They wanted me to be the assistant foreman of the Wheel Shop, but the man I was dealing with said, "No." The man at the Wheel Shop said, "I want him to be the supervisor." He was telling me this. He said, "No, he ain't no supervisor." He said, "Well, I'll make him assistant supervisor right here, right now if you say the word." He still said, "No." That was too high of a position for anybody. Rightly, I could have. Of course, I had the knowledge of the wheel and had worked there a long time. Three-fourths of my time was spent at the Wheel Shop. But I was sent to be [supervisor of] laborers in the Machine Shop.

I never thought about being a supervisor in the railroad. Nobody had ever heard of it. When I first saw him, [remember], he said that he wasn't promising anything. I thought that was kind of cold because I didn't know what I was up there for to start with. I had never thought about being a supervisor. Nobody had ever heard of it because it had never been. So it was a whole new ballgame for me. I had some other supervisors who were very good, and I had one or two [who] had to be straightened out, but most of them were very nice.

Everybody was real nice, but I had one or two [who were not]. I had one who just couldn't see a black man being a supervisor until his supervisor straightened him out. He insulted me a couple of times in front of a bunch

Roanoke Shops employees in the late 1940s. C.G. Wiley is the man on the right. *Virginia Museum of Transportation.*

of people, and the next time [he did it] I told his supervisor. We had a fire truck, to put out fires, in each shop, and that's an important safety item. Somebody had run over it and bent the tongue of the coupling on the truck. And my supervisor in the Diesel Shop told me, "Get your men, take it over to the welder shop and tell the supervisor to straighten it out. It's a safety item." I went over to the man, Mr. So-and-So, and he said, "Put it on over in the corner over there." So I told the truck driver to put it on over there and I walked away.

About three hours later, the headman asked, "Where's the safety wagon?" I said, "It's over at the welder's." He said, "What's it doing over there? I want you to get it back." I said, "I went over there and had the fellow hook it up to the truck, and I called the man's name and he said, 'Put it over there in the corner.'" So he went and got the man over him, the headman, and went over there to him and said, "Now, this is the second time that you've insulted Mr. Scott. I told you that we are a team. We've got an assembly line. The next time you insult him, we're going to be one

51

short on the team—is that understood? Now fix the thing." He said, "He's same as you. We're a team. If you can't respect him, we're just going to have one short on the team."

When I first went up there, most of the blacks got the dirty, greasy jobs. But I felt a laborer was a laborer; I don't care whether you're black, white or green. I told this fellow—he was white—I said, "Clean the pit under so-and-so engine so the electrician can get under there and work." He said, "[You want] me to go over there and clean the pit?" I said, "Yeah, go over there and clean the pit." And he went. He went out here to Williamson Road to the union office and said, "Mr. Scott gives me all the nigger jobs." The fellow came back from the union and said, "So-and-So is out there talking about his union job." I said, "What'd they say?" He said, "So-and-So said you gave him all the nigger jobs." I said, "Oh, I see."

So I went out there and said, "Come here, let's go in the office." I went in and told the superintendent what he did first, and he said, "We can't fire him because what he said was in the union office, and that's not on our property. But bring him in here—I'm going to shake him up." [The superintendent] went outside the office and called him and said, "Mr. So-and-So, were you out at the union office with So-and-So?" He said, "Yeah." The superintendent said, "What is the remark you made about Mr. Scott?" He said, "They all came back here and stretched the things." The superintendent said, "You know I don't like a liar. If you lie to me, you know I'm going to get rid of you. Now, what did you say?" He said, "I said, 'Mr. Scott gives me all the nigger jobs.'" He said, "Now, I'm going to ask you, what is a nigger job? Are you classifying that as working in the pits and grease and stuff? How much do the laborers make?" He said, "About nine dollars or something." [The superintendent] said, "Do you make nine dollars and something, laborer rate?" "Yeah." "Well, I'll tell you what, you beg his pardon now. If I hear you or anybody else…you don't know how close you are to that gate down there. You beg his pardon. Mr. Scott, you carry him out there and give him a good nigger job." That's what he told him, and I gave him one.

I had some problems; all jobs have some problems. It wasn't one that I couldn't handle. I'd give them two or three chances. He'd say, "Anytime C.D. Scott brings it to the office, you'd done had it already because he's got too much patience with you all right now. He's the supervisor, and he can tell you what to do." That cured a whole lot of problems. I had the backing. Last Friday, I ate breakfast with all the supervisors who are retired, about forty or fifty of us. I am the only black man over there right now in all of Roanoke. They treat me just like them.

I was the first black [supervisor] in the East End Shops. When I retired, [the superintendent] called one of the headmen who does the hiring and said, "C.D. is retiring. I'm not going to ask you for any particular person because you don't have any two that match up to him. Just send a man; we'll break him in." That's what he said. I'm one of the icebreakers. [We've] had two or three black vice-presidents. One of them just retired. It's changed; it's a new railroad. I enjoyed it. I enjoyed every minute of it.

Chapter 4

CARROLL SWAIN

Carroll Swain, 2013. *Photo by Art Sellers.*

Carroll E. Swain was born in Roanoke in 1927. He received his BS degree from Hampton Institute in 1953. He served in the military both before and after his degree. He was drafted during World War II and served as a military policeman in Italy for fourteen months before returning home and graduating from Hampton. Upon his return to the military after graduation, he served eighteen years and retired as a lieutenant colonel having earned two Legion of Merit Awards, an Army Commendation and a Bronze Star. He retired from the military in 1971. Mr. Swain comes from a railroad family. His father, Robert Gilmore Swain, worked for Norfolk & Western for more than thirty years as a coach cleaner. His brother also worked for N&W, as did two uncles, who performed as wheel rollers. Mr. Swain worked for N&W for a couple years during his high school years and before he was drafted. He worked in the commissary for the Dining Car Department and the Express Station as a freight handler. Mr. Swain later served on the Roanoke City Council, was a founding member of the Norfolk & Western

African American Heritage Group and was instrumental in the development of the N&W African American exhibit at the Virginia Museum of Transportation.

A TIGHTKNIT COMMUNITY

"Don't let anyone walk on you."

My father worked for the railroad better than thirty-some years. I don't know exactly how many years, but he died at the age of fifty-nine with about thirty-some years of service with the Norfolk & Western Railroad. He was a coach cleaner, as they called them. He started at that the first day, and when he died, he was still a coach cleaner, thirty-nine years later. I understand that at one point, because of his experience or time-in-grade, they made him a gang leader. This was the guy who oversaw what the others did. They may have increased his salary about $0.10 an hour at that time. I'd like to indicate that he died in 1957. At that time, his take-home pay had not exceeded $100 a month. So you can imagine thirty years ago what he started out with. As a matter of fact, my father worked two jobs. He worked on the coach yard as a coach cleaner and at the Express Station as a freight handler. He worked there about five hours a day for five days a week and then went to the coach yard and worked eight hours. That's the reason he could provide a better life for his family in the form of a house that was comfortable. I would say we lived well.

He was a good man who raised a family of two sons and bought a house. We lived in northwest [Roanoke] in two different houses. The last one was on McDowell Avenue in northwest, above Park Street. In that area, people had a tremendous amount of pride. They kept their property up. I think [more] than 60 percent of the males in that neighborhood were working for the Norfolk & Western Railroad in various capacities from brakemen down to laborer. I would say better than 80 percent of the people owned their homes in that neighborhood. From the standpoint of employees with the Norfolk & Western Railroad, I think we had two or three brakemen who lived in the neighborhood. The reason I emphasize that is because those were the highest-paid African Americans who worked for the railroad. They had the bigger homes, and most had some form of a car. At that time, most of them had Buicks. It's just the way that they lived. They also educated their kids and sent them to college.

I recall a family of Hamlars—Lawrence Hamlar, who owned Hamlar Funeral Home. We didn't live too far from them, but on a different street. I think Mr. Hamlar, who was a brakeman, educated all of his kids. He had a daughter by the name of Natalie who completed high school with me. I think she later obtained a master's degree from Howard University. There was one brother who became a dentist and another one who became a consultant in education. All the children in the family were educated in some form.

At the time, the work [of a brakeman] was dangerous, and they accepted African Americans in that type of work. In my lifetime…I recall about three cases where the brakemen lost their legs. They had a brake stick, and the wheel on top of the boxcars needed to be tightened to make stops. It might be more than one car at the time because they were forming the trains, and mistakes were made. In inclement weather, they were out during that and would slip [and someone would lose a leg]. I don't know what kind of benefits the railroad gave them, but normally, in cases of African Americans at that time, if anything would happen that would cause them to receive benefits, they were minimal. It used to be a common situation when I was working for the railroad: if you couldn't work, you were fired. That's just the attitude that you lived in at the time working for the railroad. It wasn't good.

Being a young black, what my parents taught me was: "Don't let anybody walk on you." It was quite difficult for me. I just couldn't make it. That was primarily the reason that I left the railroad in 1948 and went to college. I said, "Well, that's what I'll do. I'll just go to college." I used the GI Bill. That was the best decision I ever made in my life. Education is the reason for me being what I am today, a retired officer from the military. I worked for Roanoke City Schools for twenty-one years in a responsible position and came to [help] develop a situation where the contributions of African Americans to the railroad were recognized. I was happy when the opportunity came up.

I never will forget when Kay Strickland [former director of the Virginia Museum of Transportation] came to the city council. I was on the city council at that time. She indicated that a certain amount of money was needed for the museum, and city council had to go along with what she proposed in order to get this money. At that time, I said, "I can't vote for this because you're asking for something, and I don't see the contributions of African Americans to the railroad." The only thing that I saw at the Virginia Transportation Museum was a picture of an African American handling baggage for a white man getting off the train, and the white man was in a white suit. To me, this was demeaning to this person who was handling this baggage.

Fifty-year members of the Veterans Association, November 1, 1930. *Norfolk Southern Corporation.*

Passenger car and porter (William Taborn) in Roanoke, 1935. *Norfolk Southern Corporation.*

"Wheel Rollers" of the Roanoke Shops, late 1930s. *From left to right*: Earl Dunning, John Canty, Charles Wiley, Monk Wiggins and Thomas Campbell. *Virginia Museum of Transportation.*

I knew this man. His name was Mr. Taborn. Mr. Taborn was a leader in his church [and] a leader in the community. He bought a house and educated his kids from what he was doing for the railroad. There they had him in that demeaning position as I saw it. I said, "There he is, and you couldn't go any further." If he worked there for fifty years, he would have been the same thing after fifty years—no advancement whatsoever. Like I said, he had the qualities that benefited the black community and also benefited the city in what he was doing. There were other black men who worked for the railroad who were doing some of the same things, which were very, very important.

I began to name others, such as my uncles who rolled the heavy wheels. My uncle John Canty gained the title of "Wheel Roller of the World." I had another uncle, Earl Dunning, who was involved with that, too. They used to put on programs down at the American Legion auditorium. A lot of people used to come to see that. Also, important people who had high positions with the railroad would be there sitting in the front row looking at them. The wheel weighed over seven hundred pounds. It's amazing what they could do. In the videotape down there with the exhibit, it shows John Canty rolling the wheels and putting a little stool together, but there's something else that he used to do with the wheel. He would line up a bunch of candles on the stage or a platform and light those candles. John could roll that wheel and, with the hub of it there, the opening in the wheel, let it drop over the candle and smother the flame.

As a matter of fact, my uncle Earl Dunning used to balance a wheel and stand on top of it. Then he would come off, and they would get the wheel rolling again. He had a wire that little kids used to have little wheels that they would roll around. I think they call the wire a "scotcher." He would be up there playing like a little kid with this heavy wheel, rolling it around on the stage. The others had their show time, too, and they could do certain things. It was amazing. It was beautiful. It brought some recognition to the fact that blacks worked for the railroad. Blacks had skills that could produce better things for the railroad, but the opportunity was not there for them because they had you in a class where you were employed, and you stayed that way. You were not promoted. That was bad. In some cases, they had you training a white person, and the next thing you know he was promoted and you had to say "sir" to him. You knew that he didn't know any more than you knew about the job, but you had to say "sir."

A MILITARY MAN

"Young man, you're going to be something, and you're going to be different."

This was during the Jim Crow period. That's what I was exposed to because I first came to the railroad to work when I was sixteen years old—and only because my brother had a job at the commissary for the Dining Car Department. He was drafted into the navy, and they needed somebody to work. They let me in there to work. I was sixteen. I turned seventeen working on the job, but when school started, I quit and went back to finish up high school. I went to high school for four years. I entered high school in February, and I graduated in February. When I returned to the railroad, I came back to the Express Station because the position that I had at the commissary was filled by someone else. I worked at the Express Station for a short period. Then a position came open back at the commissary. So I went and worked at the commissary. From there, I was drafted into the army. As a matter of fact, when I came out after serving for eighteen months, I was a corporal. I went to the Express Station. I was a freight handler.

You rode a truck that would carry [the freight], and you had to help unload it at these various places because at that time, driving at the Express Station was considered a privileged job. They had no African Americans driving the vehicles, but you rode the vehicles to help unload them. That's the way it was. The tasks that they gave you—from my experience when I worked for the railroad—were demeaning. But from the standpoint of being an African American, it was the best job you could get in this city. This is the reason you hear some people say, "Well, I enjoyed it. It was good." Well, it was good because it's the only way they could provide for their family. Basically, society was such at that time that men thought different, and if you were married and had a family, you took care of the family. You stayed home. My daddy stayed home. The guys on the block who worked for the railroad, they stayed home. They raised their families. They took care of their families. The needs of the family, they provided for that. Maybe that rubbed off on me. I stayed home, too.

I only stayed [with the railroad] a couple of years. I left because I didn't see any hope to advance. I felt that I understood how to do things…and I wanted to do more, but the opportunity was not there for me to become an engineer. That was only a dream for an African American at that time. It was a good job, and [it is] what drove those men to do what they did. They recognized it was all that they could do, and they did the best that they could to take care of their families. They enjoyed going to work because of the camaraderie. I know my daddy used to leave to go to work sometimes two hours before to go down and talk to the guys, and they would have a good time. Everybody knew one another. When they got together, they seemed to be happy.

A lot of the men, you saw them in church and at the YMCA. You'd go to other meetings that they had and saw them leading in a positive direction to accomplish a positive aim. You saw them leading. These were the people who were your mentors, and you followed those people. I used to know one person who carried the name of "Mr. Monday." He was a brakeman that knew me, and every time I saw him, he used to say, "Young man, you're going to be something. Young man, you're going to be something, and you're going to be different." And I was different. I left the railroad, and I became different. I loved Mr. Monday.

[As I said], I worked at the commissary. What you did at the commissary was supply the dining cars. They had the refrigerators. They had to stock the foodstuffs. They would put in an order, and you would stack it up on the counter. The workers on the dining car or waiters and the cooks would come down and get it and place it on the train. That's what you did all day long. Then you used to have to load up stuff and bring it up to the station for trains that were coming through to put it on the dining car. You had to take the dirty linen out, count that and give them clean linen. Plates and knives, forks and spoons were normally given out by the so-called manager of that element, who was white, because those plates and knives and forks were considered expensive. At the time, African Americans were not to be trusted. That's the feeling that you had. It was hard. Sometimes you just sat down and wondered why. In other words, as a young black man, I used to sit down and wonder, "Why does this exist? I love this guy. Why is it that he wants to treat me this way? Because this is my country, I'm not going anywhere. I want to be able to contribute just as much as I can. Me contributing might help you. I love you, man." That's the way it was.

My daddy's boss was a Mr. Jennings, and my daddy used to talk about Mr. Jennings all the time. But there were certain things he said Mr. Jennings used to say and do to them that you should not do. I recall working at the commissary one night because the guy who was there for duty at night got sick, and they used me to fill in for him. My daddy used to come over to the commissary to buy milk because where he worked was not too far from it. When he came, I would give him the milk, and I would pay for it.

One night, his boss came over too and said, "I want to get some milk like your daddy." I went and got him some milk and put it up and told him, "Okay, this costs so much." My daddy walked in, and this is the way he put it to my daddy: "Gilmore, you've got a nice boy. Why don't you get him to come on over to the coach yard?" My daddy said, "What are you talking about? My boy wants to do something else. He does not want to be out there in the cold, rainy nights with the rain running down his back and through his rear end." I was just as proud of my daddy as I don't know what to say. He said, "He wants to do something else, and I'm going to see him do it"—just like that. The boss said, "You told me. That's enough." And just like that, he left. That made me respect my father more. I tell you, I loved the comments he made. That was great. I said, "God, look at my old man. He's the man now." They really didn't have the opportunity to exhibit what they were—true men making constructive contributions to society.

Chapter 5
CARL TINSLEY

Carl Tinsley, 2013. *Photo by Art Sellers.*

Carl T. Tinsley was born in 1933 in Franklin County, Virginia. Early on, he moved with his family to West Virginia, where his father was a coal miner. His mother was killed in a tragic accident, and he moved back to Franklin County in the early 1940s to live with his paternal grandparents. Mr. Tinsley enlisted in the navy when he was seventeen or eighteen and didn't complete high school. From 1950 to 1954, he served as a radio and radar technician during the Korean War. He also received his GED during that time. (He later studied at Virginia Western Community College and Shenandoah Bible College.) He returned to Roanoke, Virginia, after his service, married and worked in several jobs until he was hired as an extra by Norfolk & Western in 1957. Mr. Tinsley worked as a janitor, as well as in the mailroom and the Freight Traffic, Rate and Tariff Departments. He was the first African American to work in Freight Traffic. He retired in 1995 after thirty-eight years of *service to the railroad. Mr. Tinsley was active in the N&W union, was president of the NAACP during the 1970s, was a minister for forty years and was named Roanoke Citizen of the Year in 2012.*

An Extra Man

"I'll stick with the railroad."

I got a job as an extra man on the railroad in 1957. Black people, even working in a segregated position on the railroad, made more money than teachers. It was a good-paying job, and it was a hard job to get into. Three of my uncles worked for the railroad. Two of them worked at the General Offices. So they told me they had a job working as the extra man, and you only work when somebody's off. I turned it down at first because Yuvonne was pregnant, and I didn't want to take the chance. But the second time they told me, I went on down there, and a guy named Turner hired me.

He said, "Well, I'm going to tell you what. I'm going to work y'all forty hours a week. You can do a lot of work around here. We can wash walls, clean blinds—you know, doing all the maintenance and cleaning work." We also had a union, and the general chairman of our black union came and told us, "You can't work these men. Under the rules, you have to give the work to the oldest." That cut me back. Where I was working five days a week, sometimes I would get one day or two days. In the meantime, I had to have some more money, so I went to work for Bluefield Hardware. I heard that they had one black person working there and that he was sick in the hospital. My brother-in-law told me that he had cancer; he wouldn't be coming back, but they were holding his job. So I went and asked them for a job, and they said, "No, we're not going to fill that job because Mr. So-and-So is coming back." Well, I knew he wasn't coming back, so I grabbed the broom and starting sweeping. I really did. I told Paul Dickerson, who was the manager, "When he gets back, he can have his job. But in the meantime, you need somebody around here to do the work." I got the job. When [Dickerson] told me he was from Mississippi, my mouth fell open. Mississippi? How can anybody from Mississippi be this good? My eyes opened. You don't judge people by the state they live in; you judge them by their character. Paul was one of the finest Christian men I've ever known. I never saw him angry. He was just a good guy. I loved him.

So I was working during the day there. I'd drive a truck from Roanoke to Bluefield, load it and bring it back to Roanoke. Then I'd make deliveries around Roanoke. When I got laid off from the railroad, I got the job at Bluefield Hardware. Those are the two [jobs] I worked [at that time]. Bluefield Hardware was a job working in the day. Working extra at Norfolk & Western was night work. We had to meet the shift and be down there at ten-thirty at night. When the guy came out and called the roll, if anybody wasn't there, then the extra man would fill in his place.

We had four extra men. It was first up, first in. So sometimes you'd get work, sometimes you didn't. I couldn't let Bluefield [Hardware] go. I worked every day. And if I sometimes had a double, I'd leave N&W and go straight there and work. I worked two or three jobs for the whole time for the first few years. It wasn't that hard. Anybody else would probably tell you, "Boy, this is hard." But I didn't think it was hard work. I'd been used to hard work all my life, so that didn't bother me one bit. The guy that owned that company tried to hire me. He wanted me to quit the railroad and work for him. I wanted to be a salesman. But I told him, "No, I'll stick with the railroad," even though I had gotten laid off. This was the thing about the railroad—they hired me in September, and in December, they merged with Virginian Railway, so there was a big layoff and they kicked me out to the street.

My wife and I were gleeful over my N&W check because I was making more with N&W than I had been making the whole month at the other place. You talk about high cotton! Most the time, I'd do maybe two days a week with N&W. I'd do five days at Bluefield Hardware. H&C Coffee used to be right beside it. That was the best-smelling place you'd ever been in your life. The coffee tasted as good as it smelled.

For the first five years, I was off and on for N&W. They'd call me and then lay me off again. We had to clean the office, toilets, spittoons…oh my God, they were everywhere. When I first went there, we had thirty men working at night. We had two offices. If you ever go downtown, right across the track, we call that the "old building." Above that is the new building, and we call this the "new building." Above that is Stone Printing. We had a bathroom that we were supposed to use in the basement. Of course, you had two bathrooms on all the floors. I said, "The man must think I'm a fool if he thinks I'm not going to use the bathroom while I'm cleaning [it]."

You have to understand that back during those days, there were black jobs and white jobs. We could not apply for any white jobs because of segregation and the rules that were supplied by the company. We knew we had jobs, and they called them "cleaners" instead of janitors, doing menial work. We

Roanoke in the snow in the 1960s. From left to right are H&C Coffee; N&W Office Building South, built in 1896 and used between 1896 and 1992; N&W Office Building North, built in 1931 and used from 1931 to 1992; Hotel Roanoke; and the Motive Power Building. *Norfolk Southern Corporation.*

also had to join the union, but we had a fence around us called "class four," and you couldn't get out of that. It took us a long time to break that system down so that blacks could apply for any jobs. I was the first black to leave and go into what we called the "white world" [when I started working for the Freight Traffic Department].

If I'm not mistaken, it was 1969 when I went to Freight Traffic. I worked off and on as an extra man for five years, and then I went into the mailroom. When I got on a regular staff, the men who worked in the mailroom wore certain attire. We handled all the mail coming in, regular mail and all U.S. mail, and we made sure it all went out like it was supposed to. One of the guys that worked there retired, and I went in as an extra. When somebody didn't show up, I worked the mailroom. Well, the guy finally retired, and I got a full-time job there. It was probably around 1965.

Let me tell you the reason I went into Freight Traffic when I did. I ran the mailroom…and I had $5,000 to $10,000 a month on U.S. postage. We had these machines I had to get filled, and I had to get a check for when I went to the post office to get the machines filled. I found out that messengers—white kids out of high school—were making $200 more a month than I was. All they did was pick the mail up out of the box and take it to somebody's desk.

BREAKING THE COLOR BARRIER

"I could not hold my peace."

I met with [Richard] Dunlap, who was vice-president of coal at that time. I [said], "Mr. Dunlap, it's not fair. I've got a responsible job. I'm handling money and the company's mail, and the kids you hire off the street start making $200 more a month then we are in the mailroom." He said, "I'm going to tell Turner to go and get you boys a raise." Mr. Turner was the building manager; we worked under him. Turner comes back to me and says, "Meet me in the hall." He says, "Got you a raise." I said, "How much?" He said, "$0.03 on the hour."

Now this was before I started preaching, so you have to take it [in that light]. But I told him where to put it—where the "sun don't shine." I was so angry that I went straight upstairs to the administrator's office, and there was a job on the board as a file clerk, which paid $200 more then I was making. I said, "I want that job." I had seniority. He said, "I don't know if [they] are going to let you go." I said, "I'll tell you what. If [they] don't, I'm going to be the richest black man in town because I'm going to sue." I got the job. I went to work the next day.

From there, every time a job would come open, I'd go get a black and bring him in because at that time, they were cutting blacks off. The Freight Station was closing down, and the Passenger Station was cutting down. You had a lot of men who had been working there twenty, twenty-five years. They had the years but not the age. They were furloughed, so I'd go get them and say, "Come in here and apply for the job. You've got the time and seniority, and any dummy can do the work you had to do." They want to make us think that you can't, but anybody can file and do manual work. I think I brought in maybe six. Al Holland was one of them. My idea was that if it's going to be integrated, we need to start filling [positions] everywhere. I started it, and from there it started moving a little bit. It took a couple of years, but we had blacks in those positions. We already had one man. His name was Sam Hayes. Sam worked on the fifth floor. He was the only one they would allow to mimeograph and make the reports. He could run those machines like nobody else could.

Sam almost got me fired, though. He came down to the mailroom one day and was raising holy hell. I said, "What's wrong?" He said, "That damn railroad won't hire no black women. Tina [Harper] has been to school, takes shorthand and is well qualified, and every time she goes down there, they put her application on the bottom." Well, Sam got me hot. So I go over to the vice-president of Personnel. When I walked in, he said, "Carl, what can I do for you?" I said, "You can tell me why you don't have black women." "What are you talking about, Carl?" I said, "A woman downstairs…her application has been down there for about a month, and that guy you got down there always slips it on the bottom. We'll never get a black person as long as he's here." So the next day, Tina went to work. Anyhow, they hired Tina, and after that you would start to see a black here and there. All the guys in Personnel, as well as I, knew it. I got to know everybody there in the big shop because [I was] handling the mail for their departments. There was the vice-president and the manager, and they knew I ran the mailroom. I wasn't afraid to talk to anybody.

Al [Holland] was president of NAACP in 1970. Before his term ran out, Al resigned, and since I was the vice-president, I became president. I was the voice that spoke out. Whenever there were injustices or things done wrong, I would call a news conference and address it. I got on the railroad about them not hiring blacks. I could not hold my peace—I just really couldn't. I never started out to be a leader or a spokesmen, but I reckon because of my training in the navy and my experience in life that I would rather be dead than hunkered down under the rules and regulations of segregation. That was one thing I just couldn't do.

When I went to Freight Traffic, I went in as a file clerk. Then the job came open for rate clerk, which paid more money, so I bid on that job. You had ninety days to qualify. That was Greek to me. I'd never seen a rate before, didn't even know what a rate was. There was one guy in that place that really helped me—his name was Bobby West. With the rest of the guys, you had to try to dig it out on your own. After finding out what rates were and how they work, it was easy. Okay, how do I find these rates? Well, we had big books on it, and you had a button on your desk. You push the button, and it would turn to A, B or C. You reached your tariff to see if you could find something related, and if you couldn't, you put it back. But you had to research. I used to tell my boss, "We're losing thousands of dollars a day." That was simply because we had claims nobody could address, and after a while, you had to pay the claims off unless you could prove that it shouldn't be. I think the railroad was a very poorly run business for a long time because the only thing they thought about was coal. Coal was black gold. It was easy to handle, it came out of the mountain on the train and it went wherever it had to go—the only thing you worried about was a derail.

Mr. Dunlap used to come in at five o'clock in the morning, and you know what he better have? He better have a coal report. If the coal report wasn't there, somebody's head would roll. During that time, when I first went to work, those people would curse you out—I mean literally. It was [like that] all over the railroad at that time. It wasn't until later, after the laws were changed, that the railroad had to change their way of treating people.

Anyway, I went from Freight Traffic to the Rate Department to the Tariff Department. From there, I went to Piggyback, and then I went back to the regular General Office, where I worked as a rate maker in the plans. I stayed there until I retired in November 1995 [after] thirty-eight years of service. I have some fond memories. I'll tell you what—I loved the railroad. I didn't like what they did to me in the beginning, but I loved the railroad for what it was and for what I tried to make it. You have to understand something—unless you were part of that history, it's hard for people on the outside to look back and say, "Why did this happen, and why didn't they do something about it?" Tradition plays a big part in our life. Tradition: "This is the way it's done."

Chapter 6

J.R. HUGHES

J.R. Hughes, 2014. *Photo by Art Sellers.*

Junious R. Hughes was born in South Boston, Virginia, in 1944, and his family moved to Roanoke when he was an infant. His father was a train porter for the Norfolk & Western Railroad. He attended segregated schools, including Loudon Elementary School and Lucy Addison High School. After graduating from high school in 1962, he joined two local bands—first the Kingsmen and then the Divots. Mr. Hughes was the front singer for both bands, which were white rock-and-roll bands. However, during this time period, he also worked for N&W. He was hired in 1965 as the first black machinist apprentice and stayed through 1967. He left to pursue his dream of a career in the entertainment industry and spent years in New York City and Las Vegas. He returned to Roanoke in the late 1970s; received his BA and MA at Liberty University in Lynchburg, Virginia; and worked as a social worker, counselor and minister.

A GRAND CHILDHOOD

"[The railroad men] *gave us a cut in our strut because they demanded that you acted like somebody."*

When I was three days old, my parents moved to Roanoke. So I grew up here and had a good childhood. We were poor, but we didn't know it because the family was intact. My father, Leroy Hughes, worked for the railroad. He was a man who believed in God—not just believed but lived what he believed. He demanded that out of all of us. Out of six boys, I guess we gave my mother more headaches than you could imagine, but it was good, and the neighborhood was good. There was a beautiful little elementary school one block from my house called Loudon School. It was like a school out of a Norman Rockwell painting. Schools were segregated in those days. It was a grand place. It was a grand childhood. One block from where I lived on Loudon Avenue was where the white folks lived. We didn't go up there, and they didn't come down to where we were.

My father was a train porter and a preacher. He was a train porter for the N&W. He'd come home from work sometimes totally frustrated because some little Caucasian kid whose daddy got him a job on the railroad would have to come to my father to learn how to be my father's boss. They wouldn't let black men become conductors in those days. Train porters, brakemen, the lowest jobs—those were the jobs that black men could get. My daddy wasn't a bitter man, but he was affected by it. [Here was this] young kid, but because of the color of his skin, my father had to train him to be his supervisor. He didn't come home every day with the frustration. It was only at certain times. My father was a serious man, but he was a happy man. I think that was from his relationship with God.

Black men who worked for the railroad in this town, most of them didn't have any formal education. Working for the railroad, they could live in a pretty good home, own a pretty nice car, feed their families and take care of them. In those days, the center of the black community was the church. The men worked on the railroad, supported their families and went to church. Those men gave us—railroad men's children—a certain dignity. They gave us a cut in our strut because they demanded that you acted like somebody. That's the way we grew up because of men like Al Holland and my father. Yes, indeed. They weren't perfect men. Nobody's perfect. They gave us something in life that I don't see black children getting today. The railroad

N&W porters, Roanoke Passenger Station. *Norfolk Southern Corporation.*

Breakfast at the annual meeting of colored veterans, Ocean Breeze Beach, July 21, 1934. *Norfolk Southern Corporation.*

gave the men dignity. It gave them self-respect. It allowed them to live on the black middle-class level.

When I was nine years old, I moved off of Loudon Avenue because my mother had a baby. We moved to Tenth Street. We were the only black people in this neighborhood. I got double-barrel prejudice. From the black neighborhood I left, they resented us because we lived [there]. "You all are trying to be white," [they said.] My daddy needed a bigger house. In the white neighborhood, there was this little boy who lived on the corner. His name was Pudgy. Every day, Pudgy said, "Let's fight." I said, "Man, I don't want to fight you. My father told me not to be fighting." "Let's fight," every day. One day, we were wrestling. He grabbed me. He was like a pretzel in my hands. I could have broken him three ways. And one night, a guy shot at me, but even with all that, there was a little white boy that lived next door to us. He became my best friend. The white guys used to beat him up because he befriended me. [These are] slices of life. I was never bored.

FIRST BLACK MACHINIST

"I guess the old man is dead today, but I became one of the best machine operators on that job."

I started working with the railroad in 1965 [after the passage of] the Civil Rights Act. I was the first black machinist on the Norfolk & Western Railway. I had to take a test, and I evidently did well enough on the test that they hired me. So I was the first black machinist apprentice. I go to be with this guy for a few months and learn the job. Some of them wouldn't even speak to me. There were two old codgers in the Wheel Shop. They were cute, old white men. But they wouldn't even speak to me. The foreman came in and saw me sitting in a corner. He said, "Look man, you've got to work." I said, "Listen boss, I don't want to get those guys in trouble. They've worked here for thirty years in what they do, but they won't teach me anything. They won't even speak to me." Well, he reamed them out, and then they started teaching me the work.

A machinist primarily runs a lathe machine, which cuts metal and makes things with metal, but my apprenticeship also included being a diesel

Pattern Shop. *Norfolk Southern Corporation.*

mechanic. I went by my mother's house one day when I got off of work with my uniform on. She said, "Son, take off those coveralls and let me wash them." I said, "Mama, my wife can wash them when I get home." She said, "No, give them to me. Let me wash them." I took them off. You know what my mother did? She burned them up. "I didn't carry you for nine months," she said, "for you to be a grease monkey." She didn't tell me I needed to quit, but she said, "You need to find something else to do."

I was working third shift—eleven at night to seven in the morning. To get off of that third shift, [because] I'm young and married, I bid on a daylight job. The white guys—there were no black machinists—they were scared of this job because you had to drill through these wheels with a two-thousandths to three-thousandths tolerance from the top of the wheel to the bottom of the wheel so that it would press on the axle tightly. The wheels at that time cost about $400 a piece. If you messed one up, the boss wouldn't like that. I bid on the job [and got it].

In the safety rule book, a man is supposed to be with you for three days until you learn the job. A guy came down there and spent thirty minutes with me—not even thirty minutes—and he laughed. He said, "Well, I got to go. Good luck." I worked on that job all week not knowing what to do, hardly knowing how to cut the machine on. The man who ran that job on the second shift…you talk about redneck. This man was the father of rednecks. He came in. I said, "Mr. Smith, would you please teach me, sir, how to run this machine?" He said, "Boy, you want to learn this job?" I said, "Yes, sir. I'll pay you if you teach me this job." "You don't need no money. Get a pencil and paper." He taught me everything from A to Z how to run the machine. Mr. Smith didn't like anybody. He didn't even like his own people, but he taught me that job. I guess the old man is dead today, but I became one of the best machine operators on that job.

I made wheels in the Wheel Shop. I worked in the back with those two old, cute white guys. They worked in the Ball Bearing Shop. I worked in that. And as I told you, I worked on the diesel engines. I worked in the East End Shops. I worked at Shaffer's Crossing for six months, and I didn't like the atmosphere there. It was an open-air place. I do not like cold weather, but the guys up there were all right.

SEEKING FORTUNE IN NEW YORK CITY

"I regret leaving the railroad."

I left the railroad in the beginning of 1968 and went to New York to seek my fortune. I got my fortune, all right. When I left, even the old white guys who worked on the line above me and below me, they almost had a tear in their eyes. [They said], "Hughes, what you leaving the railroad for? You got a future." [I said], "I'm going to New York to become a singer." [And they said], "Don't do that. Stay here." The black guys, the laborers and the white guys said, "Hughes, don't do that." Those guys begged me, "Hughes, don't go, man. You got a future with the railroad." But my eyes were big. I regret leaving the railroad because if I had stayed, I would have gone up in the company, made good money and had a good career.

I even went back to the railroad when I came back from New York. I went to Mr. Hunt and said, "Listen, I want my job back." He said, "Hughes, you've been out in the music world. You've been to places I've never been to. I don't believe you want to come back down into this dirty shop and work on this filthy railroad." I said, "Yes, I do Mr. Hunt. I made a mistake." He said, "I'll tell you what. You'll have to come back down here several times to convince me that you want to come back down here." While I was thinking about going back to see Mr. Hunt again, IBM offered me a job.

This will sound strange to you, but I enjoyed my job at the railroad. [You might ask], "Why did you do that going through what you went through?" [It's] because we had a little community down there in the shop. There was a man named Mr. Moon. Mr. Moon had a little store over by where we worked. He sold cigarettes, candy—whatever you wanted. Moon was a nice man. Moon was nice to me. We had a little community of sorts down there. I'll tell you, when men would retire, they would be home for two or three weeks. The next thing you know, you see them back down at the railroad hanging around at the railroad. I remember one guy said, "Well, my wife said she doesn't want me at home under foot, so I don't know what else to do but come back to the railroad." Those guys loved the railroad.

The railroad always had an attitude of: "Black man you get back. You get the labor jobs but you don't get in the skilled professions." When I broke that as a machinist's apprentice, I paid. Like those two little old, cute white guys down in the Wheel Shop. Though they mistreated me, I just looked at them and smiled because I guess the world was changing too much, too fast for them. Maybe I didn't have sense enough to get bitter. Maybe I didn't care that much. But I look back on the railroad with fond memories. The railroad offered the black man a way to feed his family and live halfway decent in this city. Because of the railroad, my father was able to feed us and clothe us. I don't have any ill will toward Norfolk Southern. Now it's called Norfolk Southern. I have some good memories. The railroad is part of my life. I thank God for the experience, even with the race prejudice.

Chapter 7

JOHN NUTTER

John Nutter, 2013. *Photo by Art Sellers.*

John A. Nutter was born in Philadelphia, Pennsylvania, in 1948, and moved to Roanoke in 1951 after his parents divorced. He attended segregated schools in Roanoke and graduated from Lucy Addison High School in 1966. He served four years stateside in the air force during the Vietnam War. Mr. Nutter has spent his career in transportation. Between 1970 and 1987, he drove tractor-trailers, drove for Yellow Freight System and Greyhound and taught truck driving for Indiana Vocational Technical College in Indianapolis. He signed on with Norfolk Southern in 1987 as a brakeman on the Radford Division, was quickly promoted to locomotive engineer and conductor and retired in 2013 after twenty-six years of service. He served as division president of the Brotherhood of Locomotive Engineers and Trainmen for eighteen years. He is one of the founding members of Rails of Color and the CABOOSE after-school program.

Growing Up with Trains and Trainmen

"If he takes care of his shoes, he's subject to take care of the rest of the things in his life."

[My mother] worked as a domestic, and one of my earliest recollections was her working for the Union News Company in what is now the [O. Winston] Link Museum, which was the train station. And as a young lad, I used to walk from the house to meet her on what is now part of the Hunter Viaduct. I would stand there on the corner and wait for her to get off from work, and we'd walk back to the house together. But I had a reason for meeting her. I wanted to look at the trains. At that time, Norfolk & Western was still running passenger trains, and they were still operating steam locomotives, the Js. They were operating the As and the Y6s. So my earliest recollections of Roanoke evolved around the railroad and me being at trackside.

I have loved trains ever since I was an infant because back then, most of the transportation was either by rail or by bus. We did a lot of traveling by train, and Mom used to tell me that she would lay me on the seat and I would be there just as calm, listening. My earliest recollections of traveling on trains is between Lynchburg and Norfolk and looking out the windows and seeing the wisp of smoke float by and the line posts looking like a picket fence as the train traveled through the marshlands of eastern Virginia. So, yes, I've always liked trains, but I've liked anything that had wheels and made a lot of noise.

I spent a lot of time watching trains. My haunts were the Henry Street Bridge and the Fifth Street Bridge, and when I could get away with it, I would walk down to the station around eleven o'clock in the summertime and stand there and watch the trains. Those were train times because you had two trains going west, one going east and, around noon, one going south toward Winston-Salem. And you'd get to see trains from the Southern Railway and also trains from Norfolk & Western. Norfolk & Western would be running the Powhatan Arrow west, and I believe it was the Birmingham Special that was running toward Bristol. And you had the "Punkinvine" train that ran toward Winston-Salem all in there at the station at about the same time.

When I first started out in northeast Roanoke, a lot of the men worked in the East End Shops. And about six-thirty in the morning, you could hear the tramp of feet, and you could hear these men walking from northeast Roanoke, where a lot of the blacks lived, to the East End Shops. And then around seven o'clock, you could hear the whistle blow, which meant that

"Henry Street Bridge, Roanoke, Virginia," colored pencil drawing by self-taught African American artist David Ramey. *Collection of the artist.*

you were supposed to be at work. You had one or two whistles. One would blow at seven o'clock, and I believe the other one blew at seven-thirty. And sometimes you could hear people running because they knew they were getting close to being late to report for work.

When I lived in northwest Roanoke, some of the people that lived in the neighborhood worked in the dining service. You would see them leaving their homes with their grips, and they'd be walking from northwest

African American veterans meeting, Roanoke, 1936. *Norfolk Southern Corporation.*

Roanoke in the vicinity of Fifth Street, headed toward the dining car shops or commissary, if you will, because the dining cars were stored just east of where the Link Museum is now, and so was the commissary. And you'd see them. [You] didn't really know what it was that they did, but you'd see them leave, and then a couple of days later, you'd see them coming back up the street headed back to their houses. And you knew that they worked for the railroad and knew some of their kids, but they walked. A lot of them didn't own cars. They lived close enough to where they could walk back and forth to work.

When you talked to them, you always got the feeling that they were extremely proud of working for the railroad. When you heard somebody ask them, "What do you do?" [They would reply,] "I work for the railroad." There was a pride, and sometimes it was borderline arrogance. If you worked anywhere else, you didn't have a job. That was the impression I got. But the other thing that always struck me was the way they looked. Yes, the jobs may have been in service, but they were always sharp—shoes shined, clothes neatly pressed—and they carried themselves in a very distinct way. And a lot of times they had no problem with correcting young boys when they were misbehaving and would just stop you. I've been stopped on several occasions by these guys and told, "That's not the way you need to act." I have been told on occasion by some of these fellows, "You need to shine your shoes." They would tell you, "Look at you; look at your shoes." I could ignore Mom, but when a male on the street stops you and tells you that you're not presentable and that you need to shine your shoes, it sticks with you. And it stuck with me because you'd see these guys going to work with a tie on. I guess that has influenced the way that I like to present myself because one of those older fellows—I can't even remember who it was, but it stuck with me—told me that you can tell an awful lot about a man by looking at his shoes. [He said,] "If he takes care of his shoes, he's subject to take care of the rest of the things in his life."

Brakemen, Hostlers and Engineers

"This ain't my first rodeo."

So in 1987, I was looking for a job because I had a house note, two kids to raise and a wife who didn't take my not being employed as a joke. And at that time, Greyhound had changed, and I was working every day but making half the money. So I was looking for a job, and I put in an application with a unionized company in Wytheville, and I saw this cattle call for Norfolk Southern. There was an ad in the paper saying they were looking for brakemen. And I said, "Okay, I'll go down and see what they have."

I went to the hotel, and there were about four hundred people filling out applications for a brakeman's job. The job paid $75 a day. I was making $132 a day seven years ago, and I'm thinking, "$75 a day!?" I said, "There's got to be more to it than this; otherwise, who would stay?" So I made it through the entire process. I don't recall anyone ever telling me that they were going to be calling me. So I went on about my business. One day, I was at the house, and the phone rang. They asked me if I was still interested. I'm thinking, "Why would I waste a whole day and not be interested?" That was on the second of July, I believe. They said, "Well, you need to get a physical, and we need to get you fingerprinted." Nobody ever told me that they were going to offer me a job. And I'm thinking, "I never worked for a company that does things like this."

So I went down, and then I had to wait to get my physical because it was the Fourth of July. But my seniority date was July 3, 1987, and that's when I hired out as a brakeman on the Radford Division for $75 a day. However, they didn't tell you all the ins and outs of earning. It didn't take me long to figure out that for $75 a day, I may be on duty three hours [and] get called back out. That's a second day, so that would be $150. Then I found out that you could make overtime after eight hours. And if you doubled, it didn't take long for me to find out that you can make a little money. But I hedged and kept my commercial driver's license in case I didn't like it.

The job was dirty. The brakeman was the lowest member of the train crew. The conductor was his boss, and the engineers didn't think much of him. And at the time, the rail industry was going through a transition and scaling back on the number of people on the train. I hired on as a non-protected employee, which meant that there were certain payments I did not receive and that I could be furloughed [without pay].

The brakeman's job was to do whatever the conductor told him to do. He worked on the ground. You coupled up the engines to the cars, and you set cars out. And in Bluefield, at the time, all the coal trains were tied down in the yard. You'd go down into the yard. If your train was in one piece, fine. You'd get about thirty-five hand brakes off, and that was the brakeman's job. The conductor would be back there on the caboose on the rear of the train. And at the time, he either had a head-end brakeman [or] a rear brakeman. I always considered the rear brakeman as the conductor's flunky. The head-end brakeman was the slave.

If you worked with a good conductor, he would send the rear brakeman up to the head end, and the two of you would get the brakes off or do whatever was necessary to get the train built. A lot of times, the train would be in two different tracks, and you would pull so many cars out of one track and double it back over to the other track. So you may get thirty brakes off of this one track, tie up fifteen or twenty brakes on the cars that you left, pull those cars out, shove them back up into another track and make the train solid. [You'd] wait until they did the brake test and got the air pressure and put on a holding brake because the yard in Bluefield was downhill off the mountain. Then you'd get another twenty-five or thirty brakes off by hand, and you had to climb up every car, climb back down and go to the next one, knock those brakes off and then head back to the head end. And then you hoped that everything stayed together and you didn't have any problems leaving Bluefield because if the train went in emergency and lost all its air, then you had to retie the head end to keep the train from rolling so that you could pump the air.

And you did this in the summer, in the rain and in the cold. That first year, I didn't think I was going to survive. That winter was one of the bitterest winters. It snowed and snowed, and I wasn't equipped with enough of the proper gear. The next year, I said, "I'm going to have the gear to keep me from freezing out here." And after I got that gear, the second year, it was cold and snowy. Then I had spent all that money on this gear and didn't use it any more than about five or six times, but it came in handy the one night when I was out there and it was four below zero. The yardmaster wanted me to stand there where the joint was going to be made, where they were going to couple up when they doubled over and where they were shoving the rear to the train.

At five o'clock in the evening, when we went down there to the train, it was already at zero, and the temperature was dropping. He was telling me to go and stand. That was the kind of mentality that we dealt with because brakemen go down there and you wait for them. [I would think], "I can't even see where you're going to make the coupling, and you're expecting me to stand out here in this snow and the temperature dropping below zero. You're up there in the tower; you have no idea where I am. I got the radio. If you holler at me, I'll just step outside and say, 'Yeah, I'm in place, I'm in place.'" I wasn't about to stand out there in that weather.

And as it happened, about two hours went by before they shoved the train together. Then, when they tried to put the brake on, they got the pressure to make the brake test and the train went in emergency. So they had to re-pump: they had to get the pressure again [and] put the brake on again, air goes down. I'm sitting in a little shanty with the electric heat turned on. You almost think I just look dumb. But as it turned out, we didn't even leave on that train. They came back and got me. They hollered at me and told me to get up on the avenue because a ride was coming. It took us back to the top of the hill and put us on a pig train, an intermodal train. We'd been out there for four hours.

Now, the other members of the crew were getting paid initial. I get on the train, and I got a basic day. I didn't even get overtime. So we could bid on engine service jobs. A bid came up, and I said, "I think I'd like to be an engineer." So I put a bid in, and in 1989, I went to McDonough, [Georgia,] to engine school. In September 1989, I was a promoted engineer, and I worked from September into January before I bounced back into the train service. I did that a couple of years—bouncing back and forth between engine service and train service.

Train service works the ground. They do the grunt work. The engine service is engines, the engineer's job. That's a different craft. And since September 1989, I've been a promoted engineer. I was promoted into the conductor's ranks in '89 while I was training. I guess it was around 1991 that I stayed in engine service for the rest of my career—never got cut back again. So from 1991 to 2013, I ran the engines all the time.

There was probably some discrimination, but it wasn't really overt because when I hired on, I was thirty-seven or thirty-eight years old, and I would tell these guys, "This ain't my first rodeo." I was tall enough, and I would just look at you like you were crazy. "I don't know who you think you are talking to, but I'm not your dog." I was in that class of employees that was considered non-protected. But we had some younger guys, black and white, that caught a lot of grief from some of these old-head conductors and old-head brakemen. They had been bullied and treated like dogs during their career, so it was ingrained into them because that was the mentality. Your name was "Boy." "Boy, go stand by that switch." And they wouldn't talk to you; they'd say, "When I want you to throw the switch, I'll do like this. When I want you to throw it back, I'll do like that."

And then you had some guys who were great to work for and to work with. I would say, "I wasn't born knowing this stuff," and they would help you. But if you came out there and did not exhibit the type of behavior that you wanted to learn and to work, they'd give you names. Some of them carried books. [They'd say,] "I don't want this one. I don't want to see that one again. He's a dummy, lazy, don't-want-to-work switch dolly. He's a switch dolly. Stay on the engine. Don't get off."

If I was working with a new conductor, I'd say, "Look, this is the first time I've worked this job, and I'm not sure exactly what to do. But you let me know, and I'll try to get it done." And I wouldn't duck the work. We had guys that would duck certain jobs. If you got called for a vacancy that was open in Radford, guys would mark off and mark off on call. The next thing you know, you're getting called up there to drive up to Radford to work a local. So whatever I was called for, I worked it when I worked the extra list. I thought that was the only way I was going to learn these jobs.

There were some jobs I didn't like, but I worked them anyway. And when I'd get there, instead of trying to get out of work, I knew I had to be out there twelve hours. Go on out there. If we didn't put our hands on the work, it wasn't going to get done. And the longer you stayed out there, the more miserable you were going to be. So I'd just do the work. I developed a reputation that I was going to do the best that I could. Supervisors knew that if I went to Radford, [I'd stay there.] They'd ask me, "Are you going to stay up here?" "Yeah, I'll stay." [And they'd say], "Good."

And here I was doing what I hoped to do as a kid. But when I was a kid and told my mom that I wanted to be an engineer, she just looked at me like it broke her heart because at the time, a black man couldn't be an engineer. As a matter of fact, in Roanoke, a black couldn't even be a hostler. That's the person that moves engines from location to location. You may take them from Shaffer's Crossing to the station or to the west end or to the south yard. But when push came to shove, these guys would be working there as laborers, [moving] those engines. They could move them about three hundred feet, I believe. That's what one of them was telling [me]. They'd be short of hostlers, and they needed to move an engine. They could move it so many feet and stop, and then they could move it another distance and stop again. They did this until they got the engine moved to where they needed it repositioned because if they didn't stop, they were doing hostler work. That is the most ridiculous thing I have ever heard. You could be down here at the Roundhouse at Twenty-fourth Street, and you had all these engines down there. Suppose the engine came out of the shops. It needed to be moved to the ready tracks, which were west of Twenty-fourth Street. It would be in position for a hostler to get on it and take it out and back downtown. A black man couldn't do that, but if you didn't have a hostler available to move that engine from the Roundhouse to the ready tracks, you told one of these laborers who knew how to move it, who knew how to get the fires going and all this stuff. You can go one hundred feet. It was either one hundred feet or three hundred feet, but you've got to stop. Now, after you stop, you can go another three hundred feet. You talk to those guys who did this kind of thing, and they'll tell you, "I had to train a guy that knew absolutely nothing about the engine, and then he would get a job." You trained him to be a hostler so he could make more money, and you trained him.

I had an uncle, Lincoln D. Barrett, who worked for forty years in the East End Shops. [He] never rose above the ranks of laborer, but he had five sons and bought a piece of property out here in North County. All five of his sons are college graduates. He put them all through school, and two of them earned PhDs. One of them had two earned PhDs, and he just recently died. But he was a laborer. And sometimes we talk about him because he was crazy. He was only two generations away from slavery. But he worked for

Engine 1233 on the turntable at Shaffer's Crossing, Roanoke, June 1944. *Norfolk Southern Corporation.*

the railroad until he retired after forty-some years. And he would tell you up until the day he died that the railroad was a great place to work.

Al Holland, who was the same generation as my uncle, [also says] the railroad was a great place to work. Some of them started out in dining cars, and some of them started out as janitors and stayed as janitors. However, when Al and Carl Tinsley retired, they had moved from laborers to clerks. And then people like Mary Lee Cabbler came in and moved up into positions. And some of these other guys who were part of the group and are now dead—some of them died pretty young like [James] Burks—had started moving into managerial positions. Guys like Tinsley and Holland were very active in the fight for civil rights. The way they carried themselves and the way they worked [made] people start listening to who they recommended for some of these jobs. Al Holland was instrumental, along with Reverend Tinsley, in getting a lot of these guys into train service. So then it became imperative that these guys who they recommended to go into train service do their job the [right] way. You had to emulate Al Holland and Tinsley and some of those other rascals so that the door would open up for more.

I Always Wanted to be an Engineer

"At one time, it was stated that a black man would never touch the throttle of an engine on Norfolk & Western."

I always wanted to be an engineer. Operating a locomotive for Norfolk Southern was an interesting experience. During my career at Norfolk Southern, I did get a chance to do some things that I never thought I would get to do. I was once called down to Bluefield to ferry 611 from Bluefield to Roanoke. And as you know, 611 is that steam engine that was used in passenger service for Norfolk & Western, and it is on the register of mechanical marvels. It's a historic piece of equipment. And during the trip, I was agitating the engineer who was assigned to 611 during an excursion program that Norfolk Southern had in the '80s. I noticed that he was using both hands and his feet to operate the throttle. So I asked him if that was a power throttle. He said, "Yes, it is." I said, "Why you got your feet on the bulkhead and using both hands?" He got up and told me to sit down. I said, "No, I don't believe I want to do that." And in a very firm tone, he told me, "Sit down." So I sat, and I said, "I don't know anything about operating a steam engine. I'm a diesel man." He said, "I will show you."

So for approximately thirty-plus miles, I operated 611. And while I was doing that and riding through the countryside and waving out the windows and blowing the whistle, it came to me that at one time, it was stated that a black man would never touch the throttle of an engine on Norfolk & Western. I was sitting there wondering how many times the person that said that flipped over in his grave.

Then, later in my career, during the excursion season, I got to push 611 from Roanoke to Walton. So I could sit back and watch it work and enjoy the sights and the sounds. And the very next day, I got called to push it all the way to Bluefield. But before we got to Bluefield, it started to rain, and 611 began to slip, and so I had to go to work pushing it into Bluefield. Once we got it up into the yard, that engine put on quite a show for all the spectators as it struggled to drag that train up to the top of the mountain. I missed the last run of 611 in this excursion service when it ran from Bristol to Roanoke. I was called on a high-dollar train right in front of it. I did all sorts of tricks trying to get on it, but that didn't work. So I brought my double-stack train onto Roanoke ahead of 611. Then they were retired.

"Hand on the Throttle," photograph of a Norfolk Southern engineer in a locomotive cab at Oliver Yard, New Orleans, 2006. *Norfolk Southern Corporation.*

611 steam locomotive. *Norfolk Southern Corporation.*

I was fortunate enough to work on two different fall foliage excursions using Amtrak equipment and operating Amtrak engines between Roanoke and Bristol. And earlier this year, they had an employee special using a steam engine, the 630 from out of Chattanooga. I was fortunate enough to pilot that from Bristol to Radford. And so my last year on the railroad, I had some steam. The first year, the year that I was hired on, one of my earliest trips in July was an excursion trip between Roanoke and Walton and return behind 611. So I started out with steam, and I wound up finishing up with steam.

I enjoyed being a locomotive engineer. That's what I did—I operated locomotives. I was an engineer. I was proud of my profession. And yes, if anybody says I was a locomotive engineer, I won't cuss them because I always wanted to be a locomotive engineer—just like I wanted to be a truck driver. I did that. I wanted to drive motor coaches and drive for Greyhound, and I did that. I never thought I was going to be a locomotive engineer. And I'm thankful that my mother lived long enough for me to tell her, "Mama, I'm going to engineer school." And when I successfully completed that course and became a locomotive engineer, she looked at me and said, "You always said you were going to drive one of those trains, and when you told me that, [I thought,] 'I can't bear to tell him that he can't.'" She lived long enough to see me become a locomotive engineer for the Norfolk Southern Railway. I wish I could have given her a ride on a train, but that was out of the cards.

Chapter 8

BRENDA POWELL

Brenda Powell, 2013. *Photo by Art Sellers.*

Brenda A. Powell was born in Roanoke in 1953. Her father worked for Norfolk & Western for over thirty years, mainly as a porter. She attended segregated schools in Roanoke, which integrated in 1971— her senior year at Lucy Addison High School. In 1974, she graduated from Virginia Union University in Richmond with a BA in history. Ms. Powell wanted to teach upon moving back to Roanoke; however, she applied to Norfolk & Western almost by accident in 1978 and was hired. She has worked for the railroad for thirty-five years in the Information Technology Department. She started as a junior analyst and today is a senior programmer. In addition, Ms. Powell was vice-president of the Roanoke chapter of the NAACP in the 1990s.

Red Cap

"On Sundays…we would all walk down to the old N&W Passenger Station to watch the trains come in and talk to Dad for a little bit while he worked."

My father, Herman Claxton Powell, worked for the railroad for over thirty years. He was a baggage handler. They called him "Red Cap," and they [also] called him "Clax." He did a little bit of everything. He was a crossing guard because in the old days, they had to have men that actually raised the crossing arms up to let people know that trains were coming. He did that for a number of years. He was also a messenger and a janitor. So he did just about everything for the railroad. He retired from the railroad, so he was retired for a number of years before he passed.

[My father] enjoyed working for the railroad. He loved it. He never really told us stories, per se. He worked mostly the evening shift, so when he came home during the daytime, he was resting. But he did find time to be with us. And on Sundays after church, my brothers and sisters and I would all have to take a nap. And then our treat was that we would get up, put our clothes on and then all walk down to the old N&W Passenger Station to watch the trains come in and talk to Dad for a little bit while he worked.

And then we would go back in. They had a little cafeteria, and we would get free ice cream sodas from the guys that worked in there. Then we would come back out and watch more trains come in and people get off the trains. They used to have a toy train that went around the whole Passenger Station set up on tracks near the ceiling. So we would do that. That was a treat for us every Sunday to go down there and eat and talk to the guys that worked the trains and come back. There were seven of us. That was just something we did on Sundays, and then we ended up at the Passenger Station. Well, I'm so used to saying the NS, but back then it was the Norfolk & Western Railroad. We would see the Norfolk & Western security, but we didn't get to know any of those guys personally. Like I said, when we were little, my father was the baggage handler, who helped unload the baggage off the train and load the trains with the baggage. During the summer, because he worked for the railroad, we got free rides. We could ride the trains anywhere we wanted to go during the summer, and so we would take trips. We went to New York, Pennsylvania, Washington, D.C.—just about any city—because it was free for the people that worked for the railroad and their families.

Loading baggage at the Roanoke Passenger Station, August 1941. *Norfolk Southern Corporation.*

Waiting room with men's "white" and "colored" restroom signs, Roanoke Passenger Station, April 1949. *Norfolk Southern Corporation.*

[My siblings and I] didn't think that we wanted to work for the railroad. We thought it was hard work. We just didn't want to do it, and as it is, I'm the only one that ended up working for the railroad. And that was just by pure luck. I was not intending to apply or go to work for the railroad. I graduated from Virginia Union University in Richmond in 1974, and I wanted to teach. But at the time, a history position was hard to get. So I substituted for a while. I got into a program going from different classrooms and helping kids in their reading and math. Then I was a teacher's aide for a while. And all the while I was doing this, I was also working part time at Sears in the evenings. I became friends with somebody there, and she wanted to apply at Norfolk & Western for a position in Information Technology. She wanted somebody to go with her. I was just waiting in the lobby, and the personnel director came out and said, "Well, why don't you come in and take the test, too?" And so I did. And I passed, and they offered me a job.

But at the same time, I got offered a job with the school system. I had to make a choice [as to] which one I wanted, and I went with Norfolk & Western. Everybody said, "Oh, go with Norfolk & Western. It's more secure money-wise, and it's a little bit more money." That's how I ended up with the railroad. And [my friend] went to work for the airlines as a stewardess.

I started working for the railroad on August 1, 1978. I was hired as management in the Information Technology Department. I started during the strike of 1978 [the Brotherhood of Railway and Airline Clerks strike]. I was a little worried because there were picket lines, and also my father was in the union. He said, "Oh, don't worry about it. Nobody will bother you." He drove me down the first day. Behind the Main Post Office is that big, white building, and that was Norfolk & Western's computer building. And that's where I started, crossing the picket line in 1978. I stayed there in that building before they sent us out because if you were considered management or not in the union, they needed you out there to help keep the railroad running. I was there for about maybe two weeks while they orientated us, and then they said they needed more people out. I was sent over into the old General Office Building, which was converted into apartments when Norfolk & Western gave [those buildings] to the city. We were in that building in the area where they kept track of the trains. They kept track of where the trains were at all times on a big screen, and it had lights on it so that they could know where the trains were at any given time. That's when the headquarters was here in Roanoke. And the General Office Building, the main one across from the Hotel Roanoke, was where the headquarters were. But just about everybody, at one point, was out working the trains, doing whatever they could to keep the railroad going.

WHITE MALE WORLD

"Norfolk & Western at that time still was pretty much an all-male environment."

Working for Norfolk & Western at that time, there were not a lot of Afro-Americans in the office buildings. Most of them were in the unions. Most of them were messengers or working out on the tracks doing switching or unloading trains and so forth. But there were not a lot of Afro-Americans in the [General] Office Building. When I started with the railroad, there was no mention of their needing Afro-Americans. Later on, you heard through the grapevine a lot that they needed Afro-Americans, especially women, to meet the equal employment opportunity qualifications. I'm not saying that it was easy. Norfolk & Western at that time still was pretty much an all-male environment. It was basically a male [company], and so women were slowly coming into [it] because most of the women were secretaries or clerks. We were very few.

And there were very few Afro-Americans in the IT Department when I started with the railroad. There were maybe about ten of us altogether. In my class that started in 1978, there were only two of us. The others, at one time or another, quit the railroad. A couple of them have already retired because they were of age when they started. So there are only two of us left, and we're kind of debating each other on when we are going to retire. But there were only three Afro-Americans in my class when I started. It was three Afro-American women. And both of [the others], believe or not, have passed on from one illness or another. I'm the only Afro-American left from my class, and I'm the only woman from my class that's still with the railroad. Right now, in the IT Department here in Roanoke, there are only two Afro-Americans. Like I said, there's only a small group of us left here in Roanoke. And I would say we have about eleven of us that are women, and the rest are men. Most of Norfolk Southern's IT Department is run out of Atlanta now.

Being a woman, you had to kind of have a thick skin because of the language. It's a railroad, and it's mostly men, so some of the language that came out of their mouths was a little rough if you're not used to it, which I wasn't. They didn't think [about it] because it was something that they just did, and nobody ever said anything because it was always men. And so with a bunch of men, some of that language was foul, but none of it was ever—at least not around me—women-related. It was just the language that came out of their mouths. And sometimes when you were with them, they would say, "Oh, excuse me. I didn't mean for that to come out." But that's just the way they were.

But like I said, I personally have not experienced any [racial] discrimination [in my job]. I've just been in one department, and we pretty much have gotten along in my department. Other people have gone through discrimination or whatever, and they probably could tell you things. But personally, I have not felt it. A lot of it, I think, has to do with the fact that my father worked for the railroad. He was all over the railroad. Everybody knew him. And if I did [experience it], I'm savvy enough to take care of it. I know the right channels to go through to get some type of reasonable outcome out of it.

[There was] one particular incident that happened outside of work. I was at a gas station, and I was getting gas. We had just had a cleanup day at the railroad, and so I had on a Norfolk & Western T-shirt. And one of the guys—he was white—said, "You work for Norfolk & Western?" I said, "Yes." He said, "Then you must be a secretary or something?" And I said, "No." And he said, "What are you? One of the janitors or something?" And I said, "No." And he said, "Well, what do you do for the railroad?" I said, "I'm part of management. I work in the Computer Department." And he said, "No, you don't." And I said, "Yes, I do." I showed him my badge, and he said, "I didn't know that," implying that black women could be in management. It was a shock to him.

And then, after that, it seemed like whenever I would tell somebody I worked for the railroad, the first thing they would assume was that I was a secretary. I could never understand why they would assume that. Then they said, "Well, when most women come work for the railroad, they're either a secretary or a clerk." And I said, "Well, I'm not either one. I'm actually part of management." And I said my department and my title. [They would say], "You're not in the union?" "No, I'm not in the union." And I think not being in the union and being in the railroad in management shocked a lot of people.

THE CASE OF THE PAINTINGS

"Norfolk & Western—now Norfolk Southern—has come a long way."

I was also involved with the Roanoke NAACP. I was one of the vice-presidents of the Roanoke chapter in the 1990s. I'm not that much involved [now], although I am a lifetime member. But at the time, I was working with the NAACP. And it was kind of hard to step out of the role of being employed by Norfolk Southern. But I did on several occasions because as a vice-president, I was vice-president of helping people when they had a problem, when they felt like somebody had done something to them because of their race or when they felt like what was happening to them was because they were Afro-Americans.

As a matter of fact, Norfolk Southern is a Golden Heritage member of the NAACP. I was responsible for them getting the Golden Heritage membership. Norfolk & Western/Norfolk Southern, in the '70s, '80s, '90s and early 2000s, was the largest employer in Roanoke. And so we felt like they needed to belong, too. So we sent a letter. We asked, and they became a member.

[The railroad] had policies in place about racism and about how to talk to people and how to approach people. But there were always maybe one or two people that would ultimately do something. Sometimes they just weren't thinking, like this one particular instance when they bought some paintings. Norfolk Southern is good for buying paintings and then putting them in the building. And they assumed that because they had a couple of Afro-Americans on the team that bought the paintings, and because the artist that did the paintings was an Afro-American, it would not offend anyone. So they bought these paintings and put them on this one particular floor, and people would come by and say, "Oh, you need to come look at these paintings." And I did, and they were paintings of cotton fields, slavery time. They didn't think anything of it, but when the Afro-Americans that worked in those departments went by those paintings, they would make comments. And those were times that people kind of liked to forget, especially Afro-Americans, because those were not good times for us.

So they filed a complaint with the NAACP. And since I was over that department with the NAACP, I had a meeting. We set up a meeting with the vice-president of HR, and we talked about it. They really didn't think anything of it when they purchased the paintings. They thought it was okay because they had Afro-Americans on the team that purchased the pictures and because the artist was an Afro-American. I said, "Well, it's one thing for an artist to paint those. They're trying to make money, and they're trying to get their name out there. But you're putting them on a floor for people to see them, and even though we have a policy about people respecting each other and not calling each other names, it's going to come out. And if you are an Afro-American and happen to be on that floor or wherever those paintings are, it's going to affect you, and it's going to affect how you respond to other people." And they saw that. I said, "Paintings like that are for a museum or when you are doing a show, but they aren't for you to take and put on your wall in a building." And believe it or not, they took them down. So they took them down and gave an apology to us to read to the employees that filed the complaints with us.

A couple of other times, people in meetings felt like they were being disrespected because they would make comments or say something but weren't acknowledged like the others were acknowledged. Or they would say something or ask a question, and it was like they would go all around them and answer everybody else's question even though they had asked a question first. Then they would come to them and say, "Now, what did you say?" And most of the time when you were in a meeting, you might be the only one. And even though the supervisor might not think he was doing anything to that Afro-American person, that Afro-American felt like, "He's disrespecting me. He's not even acknowledging me." Sometimes you have to make them realize what they're doing.

Norfolk & Western—now Norfolk Southern—has come a long way. They've done a lot. I'm not saying they're perfect, but they've come a long way. I owe a lot of it to the people who've been in charge recently. Mr. Wick Moorman, who is the CEO now, doesn't tolerate a lot of this. His policy is that everybody be treated equal. And you don't want to let any of this get up to him. He's really tried to open the place up, [as have] the ones before him.

Chapter 9

ROBERT HAMLIN

Robert Hamlin, 2013. *Photo by Art Sellers.*

Robert E. Hamlin was born in Jarratt, Virginia, in 1953. He is part of a multi-generational railroad family. His father, James Hamlin Jr., worked for the Seaboard Coast Line Railroad, the Virginian Railway and the Norfolk & Western. His son, Ryan, has worked for Norfolk Southern as a brakeman since 2010. Hamlin retired from Norfolk Southern in 2012 after working for the railroad for forty years. He was the first African American chief dispatcher on the Virginia Division—and the only one to this day.

The Importance of Education

"You go to school, you do good work and you get good grades."

[My father did talk about working for the railroad], but he didn't talk about it a lot. I knew it was hard. I saw some of the difficulties that he went through, but it wasn't a daily conversation with him. It was a job. It was survival. And he never really wanted me to work for the railroad. He didn't even try to get me onto the railroad because he didn't want me to be on the Maintenance and Way section. He had his own reasons. He didn't want that for me. He and my mom would always say, "You go to school, you do good work and you get good grades. We're going to send you to college if we can, and you're going to do something better than this." That was the thing with my parents and me. Some of it panned out, some of it didn't—but it all worked out.

These pictures that you see out here on the section that they sell, he was one of those [laborers]. He didn't want that for me, and I never wanted it for myself. I don't know whether he knew that I didn't want that. I know he didn't want me there, and my mama didn't want me doing that either. She always preached to me. I used to hear: "Well, if I could get you in college and get you in one of those big schools, you can be president." She used to tell me that. And then I would kind of halfway buy into that because I knew I couldn't be president, but I could be somebody. And so I never really got a chance to go to college until I came up here and went part time to Virginia Western for a couple years. I'm lacking twenty-four credits of an associate's degree in business.

[I didn't go to college] because my sister went to college before me, and she's four years older than I am. She developed lupus, and my dad lost a bunch of money. So that kind of put a damper on my college career. [In high school,] I was in a program where I was primed to go to college, and I graduated with the equivalence of two and a half years of college. I had all my advanced mathematics and all my calculus. I did okay, but it's just one of those things that didn't work out. So I took a home course that, to this day, I'm not sure meant anything. But I took one and passed it, and I used it anyway.

I got a job in a factory in Waverly, Virginia, when I first came out of high school, but I thought I could do better. So I got a job closer to home at what was then the Johns Manville plant. I worked there about six months and thought I could do better. I knew my father's boss [at the railroad], and he knew me. My dad came home one day and said, "They're looking for a clerk over at Petersburg, and they've been asking about you." I didn't know that they knew me like that, but they had already checked my background and school records, and then they'd asked my dad about me. So he came home and told me to go talk to them.

And I did. I went and talked to them and had an interview, and they gave me the job on the basis that if I could learn how to do it in forty days, I could have it. I knew nothing about railroads. So I was trying to work at the Johns Manville plant and qualify for the railroad, and I just couldn't do both because I had overtime [at Johns Manville] I had to work. So I had to make a decision. I said, "Well, I've got a little saved up. I'll just take a chance." I resigned from Johns Manville and put all my time into the railroad. I squeaked by. There were no blazing colors, but I did enough to where they said, "Okay."

[I was not paid during that forty-day period.] That was the big dilemma. I had bills to pay. At the time, Nationwide [Insurance] wanted to send me to school to be an agent. But they couldn't pay my bills, so I couldn't do that. I was nineteen, and I was trying to do my own life. I was trying not to get my parents deeper in debt, so I had to turn that down. I had several people that were after me, but I wasn't looking for just a job; I was looking for the best job and the best opportunity. I had to make a decision, so I decided to go with the railroad. And that put me in a position where I had to succeed. I could not fail. I had to succeed, and I did.

At that time, [my job consisted of] record keeping and yard inventory. You would list cars in the yard. You had—and you still have it today—a thing called "interchange" from one railroad to the other. You would monitor that and keep records of that. Later, you would make a train consist of whatever was in a train. The train consist had to match the actual train, so you would make that up and give them their bills of lading, their waybills, as they called them. When I first started out, the extent of the technology was a thing called a "keypunch." It was a card that held all the manifests of the trains. When you finished keypunching them, the deck of cards should look exactly like the train as far as what was in each car, whether it was empty, whether it was loaded and things like that. I did inventory of the yard. I keypunched waybills, I did bill of ladings and I did demurrage. I worked different jobs because I had to learn a lot of different jobs to fill in for a lot of different people. Sometimes I would work in the agent's office. It depended on where they needed me most at the time. I was also an operator, and that had to do with actually giving train signals and taking what we call "train orders." All these things were new to me. It was kind of scary. I told my mom I just couldn't make it, but she didn't see it that way.

It was tough at first because there wasn't anybody else there that was black doing that. I was the first black clerk hired in Petersburg. I don't know about the rest of the area or Virginia, [but] in Petersburg, I was [the first]. The biggest part of it was that we didn't know each other, so it was difficult. I wouldn't say a lot of what was going on was racial. It was just: "I don't know you; you don't know me." And it sort of went like that. As time went by, things changed as everybody got to know everybody—things changed and got better and better. It was slow going at first.

Well, there were some things that went on. It's nothing that you could specifically put on [race]. [For example], things would go missing. [They might say], "Well, Robert did it." Things like that. One of the first things ever told to me was: "Well, if it was up to me, I wouldn't hire you. But the government says I got to." And I just said, "Well, if you stay on your side and I stay on my side, we won't have a problem." I wasn't a person that just took things. So I might have been more aggressive than I needed to be at times, but I was protective of me. But those things smoothed out as we got to know each other. It never really quite went away, but it was tolerable.

You had to have the ability to teach yourself because the people that were training you were not interested in training you. So if you didn't have the ability—and I'm thankful I did—to get right down to it and teach yourself how to do these things…it was too much. One guy had a college education, and he figured, "Well, I don't really have to go through this." And he was right. He didn't have to go through that, but I did. It was going to be the best shot that I ever had, so I did what I had to do.

My mom wouldn't let me fail. We'd have a talk every day when I came home. There wouldn't be any tears. [She would say], "You go out there, and you do what you've got to do." And that was it. I don't talk about that part because it overshadows the good part of the railroad, the good part of the job. I could name stuff that went on from beginning to end if you want to do that, but I don't like to do that because there was plenty of good there.

FIRST AFRICAN AMERICAN CHIEF DISPATCHER

"From that point on, things started to change for me."

I went to Crewe in 1985, and my career really began to take off. Crewe is about fifty miles west of Petersburg. I started dispatching there—that's where I went into a Dispatching Office. [My supervisor's] name was William Wells. And the way he treated me and what he expected of me—he actually wanted me to work for him. You know what I mean? Everything changed, and it was a lot better there. From that point on, things started to change for me. That was in 1985.

And then in 1989, we came to Roanoke. They moved all the Dispatching Offices and made them all one and transferred everybody to Roanoke. Mr. Wells retired, and my chief dispatcher now was a guy named Patterson, and he was a really fair man. He was the one that wanted me promoted. They asked me to be promoted once, but I turned it down because I didn't feel like I was ready for that step. I did my job, and I think I did it pretty well. But that was a big job. They wanted me to be a chief dispatcher.

Terry Evans, 2014. *Courtesy Norfolk Southern Corporation.*

Then, in 1998, Terry Evans came. And Terry Evans is black, which doesn't have anything to do with anything. I didn't remember him, but back in probably the early 1980s, he was in Petersburg when he was doing his training, and he remembered me. I don't know why, but he's just one of those people that just remembers stuff like that. I think I gave him a sandwich or something—I don't know. He said, "Yeah, you took care of me." I never knew what that meant because I didn't remember. But he remembered me, and so that was pretty cool. But he actually called me at home one day and wanted me to go to Bluefield to get promoted because I had really high test scores. He never let me see my test scores; he said my head would get too big. You had to take a test once a year. I took a supervisor test, and I scored what I'm told is very, very high. [Terry] wanted me in Bluefield. He said, "You stay there a year, and I'll bring you back." And so I said, "Okay." That's when I got promoted, and that was in 1998.

CHIEF OF THE CHIEFS

"That's not a journey that anybody travels alone."

[I was promoted to] chief dispatcher, and I went to Bluefield, West Virginia. I didn't know anything about the territory, didn't know anything about the people. It was a whole new experience. I did my year, and nobody called. They had me working, but they had me working two divisions. They would bring me back to Roanoke and work me on this division and then take me back to Bluefield and work me on that division. I thought, "I can't do two divisions." And so the last time they brought me back to Roanoke, I just never went back to Bluefield because I just couldn't do that.

Well, I got promoted as chief. I came back to Roanoke, and then they promoted me. It's a promotion on paper, but my title didn't change. I was the head chief, the super chief—chief of the chiefs. I guess I kind of forgot that. I was super chief, and then my assistant superintendent…we got those positions at the same time. Of course, he was supposed to be my direct boss. We were active friends. [We've] been friends since we left Crewe together, and we kind of ran the railroad together and did a pretty fair job. That was Michael Morgan, a really wonderful person. He retired soon after I retired because he had some health difficulties. I've had a few myself. But soon after I retired, I could tell he was going through a lot, and I just told him, "Man, it's time for you to come on and go home."

There is not a black chief dispatcher in Roanoke. There are some on some other divisions, but I'm the only one that's ever been on the Virginia Division. But with each person, and as time goes on, it's a little easier—less wood there to chop. In the 1970s, there was a lot of wood to chop, and by the time Evans came along, they had more advancement and more advancement. It kind of worked like that.

[My father] died in 1995, and I actually got promoted in 1998. He'd come up here, and they'd treat him like he was king. He was very proud of that. He knew that I was going to be promoted at some point. All the people on the section knew me, and they knew him. He knew everybody out there, and there were a lot of people that I worked with out there, and a lot of people watched out for me. You don't actually go on that journey by yourself because there were [other] black people out there, and I knew some black people out there who were actually watching my back to make sure I didn't make any kind of mistakes. I would talk to them on the radio. Maybe I wanted to put them on the track or something like that as a dispatcher. This is after I got to be a dispatcher, and they all knew that I could go higher because they knew my dad. You don't always make the right decision. But they knew that, and they would say, "Well, Rob, why don't we just hold onto this a minute here, and we'll just get out of your way and let you do this and do that. And we'll do it this way, and we'll come back." And these people, Herman Eggleston and all these people that were out there, would call and tell me things. And so they watched me—they watched my back. They didn't want me in any kind of situation where it would be difficult for me. And they didn't want to put me in any kind of difficult situation, and they didn't. That's not a journey that anybody travels alone. Some might tell it like that, but you're not alone. There are a lot of people responsible for me. I hope that I've done some good.

Chapter 10

DAVID COBBS

David Cobbs, 2013. *Courtesy Norfolk Southern Corporation.*

R. David Cobbs Jr. was born in Roanoke in 1956. He was raised by his grandparents Ernest and Lily Cobbs. He graduated with a BA degree in psychology from Duke University in 1978. He worked as a track laborer with Norfolk & Western in the summer of 1977 and vowed never to work for the railroad again. However, after his graduation, he decided to work for a year while deciding which graduate school or law school he would attend. He got a job with Norfolk & Western in the summer of 1978, and thirty-five years later, he still works for Norfolk Southern. Mr. Cobbs rose through the ranks rather quickly. He started as a management trainee during the strike of 1978 and was promoted to locomotive engineer, assistant trainmaster, trainmaster, road foreman of engines and, eventually, assistant superintendent. In 1993, he joined the NS corporate ranks in Norfolk as director of EEO and Manpower Planning. In 1999, he was promoted to assistant vice-president of Diversity and EEO, which is his current title.

SOUND OF THE TRAINS

"The railroad was just part of the landscape."

It's interesting we're talking about the railroad because the railroad tracks are what divided Roanoke between north and south. I think it's Williamson Road that divides Roanoke between east and west. So if you live on the north side of the railroad tracks west of Williamson Road, it's northwest. If you live on the south side of the railroad tracks west of Williamson Road, it's southwest and southeast. So if you continue beyond northwest and southwest heading west, you end up in Salem. If you continue east beyond northeast and southeast, you end up in Vinton.

We lived a half dozen blocks from the railroad tracks. Growing up, the railroad was something that I and most people who I was familiar with took for granted. It was just part of the landscape. When I was growing up on Center Avenue—it was Ninth Street and Center Avenue, probably about three blocks from the railroad—there was a bridge called Tenth Street Bridge that went over the railroad tracks and took you from the north side of the railroad tracks to the south side of the railroad tracks. [We would] go across that bridge quite a bit to play with kids over in southwest. There was a corner grocery store on the corner of Shenandoah Avenue and Tenth Street, and right behind that was the railroad tracks.

The railroad was just something that was part of the landscape and the environment. At night, you could hear the squealing from the cars humping. But it wasn't until I worked for the railroad that I realized what that sound that had been so much a part of my life actually was. It was something that, from my earliest memory, was always there. You'd hear the rail cars banging around or you'd hear the squeal of the brakes as the rail cars were coming down the hump. It didn't alarm any adults, and we kids took it as being something natural.

My earliest work experience was with a program called TAP, which still exists in Roanoke. It's called Total Action Against Poverty. I don't know if they considered us underprivileged, but the program exposed us to work of some sort. I was in the TAP program when I was in junior high school, and I actually worked as a janitor, custodian and handy-person assisting the janitor at Lucy Addison High School during the summer. My grandfather worked custodial jobs. He had a number of companies that he worked [for], and periodically he would take me to work with him. Before I was able to

Aerial view of Roanoke, 1936. *Norfolk Southern Corporation.*

"Scenes of Roanoke, Virginia, circa 1950s," colored pencil drawing with pastels by self-taught African American artist David Ramey. *Collection of the artist.*

drive, I learned how to travel around Roanoke using the public bus system. That was the way we went there.

One of the offshoots of integration is that a lot of the businesses in the black community ended up closing down. There was a movie theater called the Virginia Theatre, which was located off of Henry Street not far from the Hotel Roanoke. That's where you went to see all the movies before integration. Once integration came in, the Virginia Theatre closed. There was an American Theatre downtown, which I think is now closed, and there's a Grandin Theatre out in southwest Roanoke. I would use the bus to go to places like that. My grandfather didn't drive, so when he went to work, he went by bus, and sometimes he'd take me with him to help. A lot of times, I think he took me with him just to get one kid out of my grandmother's hair. I'd sit around in the offices and help him when he wanted to be helped, and I would sit in the corner out of his way when he didn't need me to help him. So between the work with my grandfather and the job with TAP, that was my first job.

Norfolk & Western

"I'm not going to make a living using my hands. I'm going to make a living using my head."

I had a used 1962 Chevy that my grandfather bought me one summer during college, and at some point early on in the summer before my senior year at Duke, I drove to Roanoke. One of my friends said that he heard that the railroad was hiring. This was the summer of 1977. I had grown up around the railroad, so I had paid no attention to it; it was just part of the landscape.

I remember it was a Friday when I went to the building that the Virginia Museum of Transportation is in now. That used to be the headquarters for the Engineering and Maintenance and Way Departments. I somehow found the office—I think it was of the division engineer. I said, "I understand that you're looking for summer help." And I met a gentleman named John Townsend. His title was track supervisor or track foreman. He said, "Yeah, we're hiring."

He asked me about myself. I told him I was in college and was going to work for the summer. He said, "That's fine. You sure you're going back to school?" I said, "Yes." I forget what the time frame was—it was either sixty days or ninety days—but he said, "We can't work you any more than that because after that, you'd automatically go in the union, and this is just a temporary position. So don't think you're going to come out here and work out here permanently because you're going to be cut off." I said, "That's no problem because I'm going back to school." So then he said, "All right." I said, "When can I report to work?" This was Friday. He said, "Well, come back here Sunday about four o'clock in the afternoon. There will be a bus here, and we'll take you to your work site. And make sure you bring steel-toe safety shoes and enough clothes to last all week." That's when I found out the position was a track laborer position. It was called an "extra force gang." It was a gang of track laborers. This gang traveled different places on the N&W system one week at a time, or sometimes they'd stay at the same location for multiple weeks. But the job was you'd work four days, ten hours a day. You had Friday, Saturday and Sunday off.

I decided I was going to follow the vehicle down. I forget how many people were riding in the bus. There were a couple of guys in trucks or cars, but it was like a caravan of us driving down 220. We ended up in a place called Pine Hall, North Carolina, and we ended up driving back on dirt roads and winding around. Finally, we ended up near a set of railroad tracks, and there were camp cars. Camp cars are railroad boxcars that have been converted into a lodging facility for railroad employees. They've got electricity that you can plug up there. And as track laborer, you stayed at this location and slept on the camp cars. They had a dining car that was attached. And so they gave me a bunk in the camp car. I got up on Monday morning. Breakfast was going to be at six o'clock, and we were going to be out to the work site by seven o'clock.

I found out that they had hired three college kids. The first thing that John Townsend said when he gathered us college kids together was: "This breakfast was pretty light. I had to prepare it. Our cook bid off the gang and moved to another gang. I'm looking for somebody to volunteer as a cook." And it wasn't David or [the kid from] Virginia Tech, but the third guy raised his hand real quick and said, "I'll be the cook." And I'm [thinking], "Gee, he was quick to volunteer." Well, I found out why he volunteered so quickly.

We have the breakfast, we get on the bus and we drive some number of miles down to another set of railroad tracks and meet up. There are other buses, and there are a number of gangs. I found out that we were going to build a spur track from scratch, from the main line to a new industry, a pipe company called Pine Hall Pipe Company. They wanted railroad service. So our job was to lay railroad tracks from the main line. I think it was about a mile and a half into this facility.

One of the notable things I remember is that every morning started out with a prayer at breakfast, with the foreman, John Townsend, reading a verse from the Bible and then reading a safety rule of the day. The other thing that Townsend had given me on that Friday was the safety rule book. He said, "You need to read this by the time you come back." I took it home and, being a studious person, read through it. I had no idea what it was saying. It would talk about rules, and it would talk about switches and frogs and things like that. And to me, a switch was something that my grandmother made me go out in the backyard and grab when I hadn't been good, and a frog was an amphibian of some sort. But these are all railroad terminologies.

This work, when we got out there at Pine Hall to do it, was hard manual labor in 100-degree temperature. That's the ambient temperature. When you'd get in between the rails, it was 110 or 120 degrees. The men who were on this gang…there was a guy named Archie Moore, who was black, and another guy named Tony. I don't remember Tony's last name. He was white. They were both from Martinsville. They drove down there together. They were best friends. Tony looked like he was as old as my grandfather, and Archie didn't look like he was much younger than that. They said, "College boy, just do what we tell you, and you won't get hurt. The last thing anybody wants to happen out here is for you to get hurt." I mean, this was like, "Hit this spike!" and "Haul this bucket around!" I had never done any hard labor in my life, and I was soaked with sweat after less than an hour on the job.

And it got to a point that by about noon on that first day…I remember holding a hammer, and I had struck a spike a few times, and we had driven a spike in. I was going to set the hammer down, and my fingers had cramped up so that I couldn't even let go of the hammer. I had to say to Tony or Archie, "Can you take this hammer out of my hand, please?" They did that. And then one of them said, "Son, you need to go to the bathroom." I said, "No, sir, I don't." "No, you don't understand. You need to go to the bathroom." I said, "What do you mean?" He said, "Just tell the foreman that you got to go to the bathroom. Walk up the tracks there. Find some place and find some shade and cool off before you come back here." And I said, "Okay."

I walked up to Townsend. I said, "Mr. Townsend, I've got to go to the bathroom." He pointed. I think he knew what was going on. I walked up the track and went around the curve where I was out of sight. It was on an embankment, and I remember sliding down the embankment on my rear end and just laying there, saying, "Oh God, please, please, please. I can't do this."

Laying track. *Virginia Museum of Transportation.*

And so I rested there. And I got back up and came back, and then Townsend said, "Why don't you go to the bus, son, and just rest? You can't do everything all in the same day." So I went back to the bus, and I was lying there. And the kid who said he was going to be the cook—who turned out to be a horrible cook, and nobody liked him because he couldn't cook…but I remember him coming on the bus because he didn't have to work manual labor. His job was to cook the breakfast, cook the lunch, bring it out the gang and go back and get ready for dinner.

So this was after lunchtime. He had come back to get some of the supplies he had left for lunch. He found me there on the bus and said, "Are you all right?" I said, "Man, yeah, but Townsend told me to come down here and just rest." And he said, "I guess whoever has you is going to win the pool." I said, "What are you talking about?" He said, "Oh, they've got some kind of wager going on of which of you college guys are going to be the first to leave." The other kid was white. He was red haired. I think he had played athletics. But anyway, the money was on me, that I wasn't going to last. I didn't even give that a second thought at that point.

When we came back at the end of the day and got to the camp cars, I said to Townsend, "My folks live in Winston-Salem. It's less than an hour from here. Do you mind if I drive there? I didn't bring enough clothes to last me for the week. I'll come back in the morning." He said, "Yeah, sure."

So I drove to Winston-Salem. When I got there, I pulled in the driveway. My mom comes out, and she looks at me and starts crying. And I mean I am stiff—I've still got cramps. And she said, "What in the world…what happened?" I said, "It was my job at the railroad." And I went in, took a hot bath and then lay down on the couch, hardly able to move, just in pain everywhere. I was thinking, "God, please take me now." My stepfather comes in and says, "You're not going back out there. I'll find you something else." So I'm sitting there, and I'm thinking, "Man, they bet on me not making it." And I decided I would go back out there. So I got up early the next morning. I remember leaving at five-thirty in the morning. My mom comes out and says, "Where are you going?" I said, "I'm going to work." And to make a long story short, I went back out there and stuck it out.

Two things came out of that. One was that I didn't appreciate anybody selling me short. So I was determined that I was going to go out there and contribute. By the end of the summer, I was in the best shape I'd ever been. I was thin as a rail but very muscular. And the other thing was that I realized I had a much greater appreciation for my grandfather. Now, he didn't do work nearly that hard, but some of the stuff he did as a custodian and a janitor—it just cemented in my mind that I'm not going to make a living using my hands. I'm going to make a living using my head. I went back to Duke committed to making the best grades that I could make. And as a result, I ended up graduating from Duke with honors.

And a Career Was Born

"I learned the heart and soul of the railroad from that experience."

Now, the other thing that I had committed to at the end of the summer of 1977, when I finished the track laborer job, was that the railroad would never see me again. I had done my time on the railroad. I made that vow at the end of summer of '77. Now we're in spring of '78, almost summer. I've graduated from Duke, and I'm trying to find employment for a year to figure out what I want to do with my life. So we've sent out all these résumés, and while we're waiting, I decide I'll go to Roanoke and spend some time with my grandparents.

When I go there, my grandmother—one of her skills is life managing; she manages everybody's lives— says, "What are you going to do now? I thought you were going to law school." "I don't know, Grandma. I've got a lot of options." "I don't see you exercising any options. What are you going to do?" I said, "Well, I'm going to work for a while." "Well, go to the railroad," she said. "Grandma, no. I had enough of the railroad." My grandmother, who apparently knew more about the railroad than she'd ever imparted to me, was just so impressed that I had gotten a job with the railroad the summer before, and she always talked about what a great company Norfolk & Western was. So she was ecstatic about that. She also had the skill that she could nag you to death. I think that she could probably nag the skin off of a piece of chicken instead of having to cut it off herself. Finally, just to placate her, I said, "Okay. Grandma, I'm going down to the railroad. I'll put in an application. I don't really want to work there. That was the hardest work I ever did in my life."

So I went to the office building, which was General Office Building South, right across from the Hotel Roanoke and where the corporate headquarters was. I put on a nice suit and tie and went down there, and I went into the lobby and was looking around trying to figure out where to go to fill out an application. And as I'm standing there, a guy comes in, also in a suit. His name was Dale Mullen. It turns out Dale was the college recruiter for Norfolk & Western. And he sees me there and says, "Can I help you?" And I said, "Yes, I'm here to fill out an application." He said, "Okay. What kind of job are you interested in?" I said, "I don't know, whatever might be available." And he said, "Well, tell me about yourself." I said, "Well, I just graduated from college." "Where'd you graduate from?" "Duke." "Okay." I said, "I worked last year as a track laborer." "Oh, you've got some experience." I said, "Yeah, I worked as a track laborer." So he said, "Okay. Well, wait here for a second."

So he goes into an office, and he comes back out and he says, "Come with me." And then he takes me to the Passenger Station Building, which is now the O. Winston Link Museum in downtown Roanoke. He took me to George Gearhart's office. He was the general manager of safety and was the person who headed up the management training programs for Norfolk & Western. So I'm in this large office sitting across from Mr. Gearhart, and he's got this big map behind him that shows the whole United States and also shows where the Norfolk & Western railroad tracks are operating.

And to me, the railroad had been Winston-Salem to the south, Pine Hall and Roanoke. I had worked up as far as Shenandoah, Virginia, so I knew Harrisonburg and those places. And then I see that there are places like Chicago and Cleveland and Buffalo and Detroit on that map—all places that looked attractive to me.

So he basically interviews me and says, "The job we have is a management trainee. You'd be an operations supervisor. You'd have to move around. We move our people around a lot. Do you mind moving?" [I said], "No, I don't mind moving around at all." And I had a long discussion with him, went home and told my grandmother, "Hey, not only did I fill out an application, but I got an interview." I didn't think anything about it, and then Dale Mullen calls me back probably about an hour after I'd been home and says, "Would you like to come to work?" And I [thought], "Well, you know what?" I didn't have any other job prospects, and I kind of liked the idea of maybe moving to one of those locations. So I said, "Yes, I'll come to work." And on July 9, 1978, I started.

[I began during the Brotherhood of Railway and Airline Clerks strike.] Well, to make this long story shorter, that strike lasted eighty-eight days, and that short train ride that we were going to take to South Lorain, Ohio, lasted about eighteen hours before we got back to Bellevue. I spent the first two weeks working with Wes Brown, the safety superintendent, as the railroad brought in management people from all over the system and sent them out of Roanoke to different places across the railroad to keep the railroad operating. After two weeks of working with Wes...they needed engineers to take trains from point A to point B. So we were taking trains from Bellevue to Buffalo, spending the night in Buffalo and then bringing the trains back to Bellevue, taking an inordinately long period of time to get there. It was the best learning experience that I could've had. I got to learn the railroad. I learned from the ground up as a track laborer, but I also got to learn hands-on what a conductor does, what an engineer does, what a car repairer does and how to give an airbrake test. I was learning a lot.

It got to the point where Wes...now imagine this—here's a kid right out of college, no experience on the railroad, and he says, "You want to sit in the seat?" Can you imagine the pilot saying to some kid with no flying experience, "Hey kid, do you want to fly this plane? Come on up here. I'll show you how to do it." I mean, that was what it was akin to. You had people who were inexperienced. After about three weeks, they decided that they were going to give people time off. Wes didn't see his family for three weeks straight.

I didn't need or request any time off. To me, this was fun. I was learning. So when Wes took his time off, they put me with a guy by the name of Ernie Freitag. Ernie was a supervisor in the locomotive shop there at Bellevue, didn't know anything about running trains along line of road. He was what they would call a hostler. He could move engines from one track to the other, but that's about all he knew. But he had that level of experience, and they decided that while Wes was off, they would pair me with Ernie and we would take a train from Bellevue to Buffalo.

Ernie could not operate a train. We stopped because the brakes went into emergency probably a half dozen times. There are metal fasteners—they call them knuckles—between the railcars, and if you don't handle the train properly, these metal fasteners will break. It will cause the air to release on the train and set the brakes, and to replace those knuckles, which weigh about eighty pounds, you have to carry them from the front of the train to wherever the disconnection is. I changed two knuckles with Wes Brown during the three weeks that I worked with him and Harry McKelvey. I changed six knuckles on that trip from Bellevue to Buffalo. It took us about forty hours to go that length of track. Ernie was a great guy. He reminded of me Hoss Cartwright from *Bonanza*. I mean, he was a great guy personality-wise. But he knew nothing about operating a train. I don't know how many trips I had worked with him when I heard Wes on the radio again and realized that he was back. But they didn't put me with Wes; they left me with Ernie. And then I realized that they decided they were going to keep me with Ernie.

Well, after another trip where I changed a lot of knuckles for Ernie, I came into Bellevue. At this point, I am ticked off, and I want to tell this guy he doesn't know how to operate a train. But I just don't want to change any more knuckles. So I march up to the superintendent's office, and there is B.J. Hoops, the superintendent. Now, he's got the railroad map in his office, but he's also got the Confederate flag hanging on one side and the American flag hanging on the other side. I walk in, and he said, "Hey there, Management Trainee Cobbs. How you doing?" I said, "I'm fine, sir." He had a couch in his office, and another guy is sitting on his couch. I didn't know who he was, but it turns out he was the railroad general manager. He was Hoops's boss. But as far as I was concerned, Hoops was the boss. He was the only person. This guy always sat around and was very quiet. He said, "Who you working with now?" I said, "I'm working Ernie Freitag." "Oh, you're not with Wes anymore?" "No, sir." "What can I do for you?" I said, "You need to make me an engineer." He said, "What?" I said, "I have changed about ten knuckles with Ernie Freitag on my trips. Wes Brown showed me how to operate a locomotive and handle a train. I can do a better job than Ernie Freitag. Either you make me an engineer or you just send me home." He looked at me and said, "Okay. I can see you're riled up about this. Why don't you go on over to the dormitory and take your rest, and then we'll see what we can do."

The railroad at that time had lodging facilities on their properties. So when I was at Bellevue, I stayed in what they called a dormitory. The picketers were off the property, so we were sequestered. They were actually helicoptering people in. They would fly people into Cleveland or into Sandusky, Ohio, and then they had helicopters that would fly them in to avoid the pickets.

The rule at that time was the hours of service law. You weren't supposed to work over twelve hours, and you were supposed to have at least eight hours rest between trips. Well, we were violating the hours of service law like you couldn't believe, but they were giving us that minimum eight hours rest between trips. It was like clockwork. Regardless of when I ended my tour, about seven to seven and a half hours later, they were calling me to come back to report for duty when the eighth hour had elapsed.

So I went back to the dormitory, and I thought, "You fool, what did you just do? You just went up there and made an ultimatum to the most powerful man on the railroad and told him to make you an engineer or send you home. They're going to send you home." I was tired. I rested six hours and then woke up. Nobody had called me. They had a restaurant in the dormitory, and I got something to eat. So now eight hours had elapsed. I hadn't been called. Nine hours, I hadn't been called. And then it cements in my mind: "Okay, you're fired. You just blew this job. You have to decide what you want to do." I'm thinking, "Can I still get into law school? What am I going to do?"

I think about ten hours elapsed before the call came. "Mr. Cobbs?" "Yes?" I said. "We got you called for whatever train. I need you to come over here at such and such a time." "All right, I'll be there." So I'm thinking, "Okay, at least you still have a job." And I walk over to the office building or go to the caller's office and tell them, "I'm Cobbs. Who am I working with tonight? Am I working with Ernie Freitag?" He said, "No, we got you with Mr. Harvey." "Okay. All right. So where is he?" He said, "Well, he'll be here in a second." So I wait around.

Then this guy named Anthony Harvey came up, and [the man at the caller's office] said, "Mr. Harvey, Mr. Cobbs; Mr. Cobbs, Mr. Harvey.

You guys are on such and such train, and you're going to take it out to wherever." And I said, "Okay. Well, all right. How long have you been operating trains, Mr. Harvey?" He said, "Operating trains?" I said, "Yeah, how long have you been out here running during the strike?" He said, "Well, I just got out here." I said, "Okay." He said, "Yeah, I actually just got off the helicopter about a half hour ago." I said, "Okay. Well, how much experience have you had operating a locomotive?" He said, "None, I'm in the IT Department." I said, "What?" So I looked at the caller and said, "Who's the engineer on this train?" He said, "Well, they've got Cobbs down here as the engineer." [I'm thinking,] "Wow! My ultimatum worked." So I ended up being a locomotive engineer. I've got all sorts of strike stories that I could tell you, but I'm not going to tell you. I ended up being a locomotive engineer as a management trainee. I ended up working the eighty-eight days of the strike.

I met some great people and developed some really good relationships with the folks that I was working with in that strike. I learned the heart and soul of the railroad from that experience. Tony Harvey was a Bob Seger fan. I remember we had a transistor radio that we would listen to. [One time] we were going through Cleveland, and he found Bob Seger on the radio. For some reason, he loved Bob Seger. I had never heard of Bob Seger before that. I worked with a guy named Emory Winstead. I forget what department he was in, but he had never been out of Roanoke before. He had a little boy who was about six years old, and he had never been away from his kid in his life. I remember we had stopped somewhere, and he was using a payphone and called home to his son, and he started crying. He looked more like Hoss Cartwright than Ernie Freitag did, and to see this big guy with tears coming out of my eyes, saying, "I miss my little guy." I'm [wondering], "What in the world?"

When the strike was over, I went back into the management-training program, which involved us going around to different departments and traveling to other locations. I thought, "Maybe I'll just stay and see how it goes. I kind of like this." And I said, "Instead of just staying for a year, I'll see how my career progresses." I put mental checkpoints in my mind and said, "If I've progressed to this point by this time, I'll stay. If I haven't, I'll explore something else." I was always able to get to that checkpoint either on my mental schedule or ahead of it. And so that's how I ended up staying around for thirty-five years.

VALUES AND EXPECTATIONS

"The Al Hollands of the world...blazed the trail."

I'll be honest with you—personally, I haven't experienced much discrimination or racism in my career with the railroad. From the earliest days when I was in Chicago, I remember a guy making a racist comment because he didn't know I was around and the other people in the room getting quiet. But I handled the situation by saying to the guy, "What did you mean by that?" and just talking through it. I didn't get upset. I realize that discrimination and racism exist. It's been my goal, even through this process, to get people to realize it's all about how we interact with each other, particularly in the workplace. We have certain values and certain expectations of behavior at Norfolk Southern. I've often said, "I don't care how you act when you're not at work, as long as you act like you're supposed to when you're at work."

I really don't know if race was ever a factor in somebody's view of me. It didn't matter to me because I felt that my performance would dictate what happened. I didn't put up with anything. If I saw it happening, I wasn't bashful about handling it. I think people respected that.

Diversity Council, Norfolk Southern Corporation, 2011. *Norfolk Southern Corporation.*

The Al Hollands of the world, and the Archies and the Tonys—I think that they blazed the trail. They put up with stuff that I probably wouldn't have been able to put up with. By the time I got here, for the most part, it was accepted that if you were black, you could make it. I think that's why I've been successful, why Terry Evans has been successful and why any number of African Americans out here have been successful. There was a guy—he's deceased now—in Roanoke [named] Jim Burks. When I started with the railroad, he was already working in management in the corporate offices in Roanoke. I might have been one of the first African Americans that the railroad sent somewhere, but I wasn't the first. There was a John Eaves who was a trainmaster in St. Louis. There was a Michael Simmons who was a trainmaster in Sandusky, Ohio. There was a Dennis Wimbush. There were people who had gone out there before I had. And those are just my contemporaries. But again, there were the Hollands and the Richard Deans and the people who really blazed those trails. They put up with a lot to make a way for their families and to make the way better for me.

Chapter 11

CLAUDE PAGE III

Claude James Page III, 2013. *Photo by Art Sellers.*

Claude James Page III was born in 1963 in Long Island, New York. His parents moved back to Roanoke in 1966, and he grew up in Roanoke and currently lives in the city. He was raised in a close-knit family and attended integrated schools. His grandfather (and namesake) was a railroader and worked forty-eight years for Norfolk & Western as a laborer in the East End Shops. Mr. Page received his BA in psychology from Winston-Salem State University in 1985. He has worked for Norfolk Southern since 1987. In his twenty-six-year career with the company, he has held the positions of brakeman, conductor, locomotive engineer, yardmaster and road foreman of engines. He held management positions for thirteen years and is currently a locomotive engineer. Mr. Page is involved with the mentoring programs Rails of Color and the CABOOSE after-school program.

Grandfather Page

"Then you would hear [the whistles] *again in the evening, and you knew Grandpap was coming home."*

My grandfather Claude James Page worked for what was then the Norfolk & Western Railroad for forty-eight years. I can remember, as a child, my grandfather getting up real early in the morning, going to work and then coming home in the evening—day in, day out. I don't think he ever missed a day or even complained about being sick or tired. He walked to work at the East End Shops in the summer, in the winter and in the rain, snow and sleet. It was just what he did, and he never was late. I remember not knowing how to tell time but knowing that you could hear the whistles from the shop. In the morning, they would sound off, and you knew it was time to go to work. You'd hear them at midday, and it was lunchtime. Then you would hear them again in the evening, and you knew Grandpap was coming home.

During that time, there were not a lot of jobs that African Americans were permitted to do, and most of the jobs that they were hired for were just laborers. That's what [Grandpap] was: a laborer. And he did that for forty-eight years. He did a good job. He had opportunities at times to train other workers, but management wasn't an option for them at that time. He never complained. He just went about his way and did what he was asked to do.

He used twenty as his age when hired even though he was only nineteen. He was born on February 20, 1900, so he started his service in 1919 and retired in 1967. I do remember that when he retired after forty-eight years, his health was good. Other family members wanted him to go the other two years to get to fifty, but he was ready to retire. Those types of things—like getting to fifty—didn't mean a lot. That wasn't what drove him. It was just a good day's honest work, and that's what he always did. Those are the examples that he left and instilled in me.

Today, you have an application and a human resources department. You submit an application, you go online and then you wait to see if your application is pulled. But back in those days, it was based on a man's word and in the work that he was doing. My grandfather obviously did a good job, and the people that he worked for were impressed enough in his work that he was able to bring his brothers on. Three or four brothers of my grandfather's were hired on the railroad based on my grandfather's work and his word.

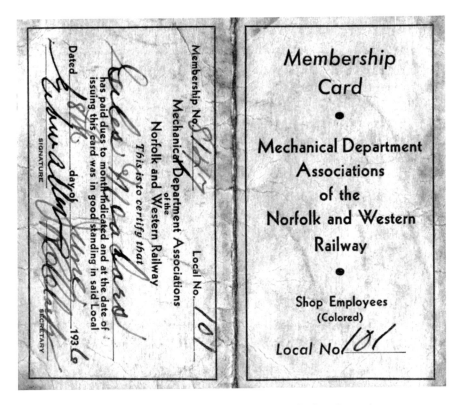

Shop employee ("colored") membership card, 1936. *Norfolk Southern Corporation.*

Through his efforts and work, he was able to own a home for my grandmother and him to live in. They raised my father and my two aunts. All of them went to college and were educated, and he was able to afford to pay for that. So even though the salary, at that time, was nothing compared to what we make today, they were able to do anything they wanted to do.

POWER OF MENTORS

"It gave me a different perspective of things."

All through college, I used to work part time at Belk [Department Store]. I remember one day this man came into the store looking for a tie, and during our conversations, he told me that he worked for Norfolk Southern. I told him I was a senior in college. He said, "Well, here's my card. When you get out, you give me a call." So I put the card in my suit coat, and I didn't think any more about it. I said, "Okay, he was just making conversation." So, I was sitting at a funeral right after I graduated. This would have been in 1985–86. I finished in December 1985, but I didn't march until '86 because they didn't have a December graduation. So I was in the funeral, and I put the program in my coat pocket, and there was this card. So I said, "Well, let me call this guy and see what he's talking about," not thinking that it was going to be anything. So I called Mr. W.C. Violett. He remembered me just like it was yesterday, and he told me what to do. So I applied for a job in sales at Norfolk Southern. I went down there, got the application, filled it out and turned it in. About two weeks later, I got a letter that said, "Thank you for your interest in Norfolk Southern. However, at this time, we're not hiring anybody right now." And that was it. So I thought, "Okay, let me call this guy up." I called Mr. Violett, and he told me to come down to his office. I went to his office, and he made a phone call. The next thing I know, they told me that there was a sales job in Norfolk. "They need you to be ready to go down there the following week and interview," he said.

My father and I went to Norfolk, and they put us up in the hotel. We got down there and got ready, and I did some research so I could be ready for the interview. I went over there and interviewed well. I think Mr. Violett was just as disappointed as I was that I didn't get it. They had some people that were already employed at Norfolk Southern, and they just kind of moved them. And then there was a grandson involved, and he got it. He told my father and me what happened. He was really upset about it.

It gave me a different perspective of things. When he first told me he was going to help me, I thought, "Okay, right." But he really tried. Then, even after that ended, he kept in contact with me. He called me the next year and said, "Look, they're getting ready to hire some brakemen. Now, I know this is not what we talked about earlier, but just to get you an opportunity to get your foot in, let's try this. And if you don't like it, you don't like it."

I went down there. The Roanoke Civic Center was packed. There were hundreds of people down there. I filled out the application. They already had a file on me from that earlier application. So I got hired in June 1987. At that time, it wasn't the Virginia Division. You had Roanoke Terminal, the Radford Division or the Norfolk Division. I got hired at the Roanoke Terminal. By October, I was going to engineering school in McDonough, Georgia, because they hadn't hired any engineers in the Roanoke Terminal

Ben Finelle, Norfolk Southern employee, 2004. *Norfolk Southern Corporation.*

for some period of time. So in a matter of about six months, I went from trying to become a brakeman to trying to learn how to run a locomotive.

Anyway, Mr. Violett and I became really good friends—not because he was white, but we just became good friends. He invited me over to his house. I had been over there to watch football games throughout this whole process from the time of getting the rejection letter, [getting the sales contact] and getting hired. We stayed in contact. A few years after that, he retired and relocated to South Carolina. But we even kept in contact when he moved to South Carolina.

My first management promotion came in 1993 in Norfolk as a yardmaster. At that time, I was married, and we moved in '92 to Norfolk. I was down there working as a locomotive engineer and conductor as needed, and a man named John Moses helped me. He was already a trainmaster. We had some conversations, and I shared with him my education. So he said, "Well, give me your résumé, and I'll see what I can do." Mr. Moses was very instrumental in getting me into the management side because I was sending things in and was either getting no response or the general "thanks for the interest" [letter]. Mr. Moses was able to get my application in, and in turn, I got promoted. He was a trainmaster, and he was an African American.

TWENTY-SEVEN YEARS WITH NORFOLK SOUTHERN

"I think about it every time I run the engine."

I'm now celebrating my twenty-seventh year with the railroad. I had an opportunity to work in a lot of different capacities. As I said, I hired on as a brakeman and then a conductor. And I was shortly promoted to locomotive engineer in the Roanoke Terminal. Then I moved on to engineer on the road at the old Radford Division. Shortly thereafter, I took a transfer to Norfolk and was promoted to yardmaster, my first managerial position. I worked in Norfolk for about four years and received my second promotion to road foreman of engines. I worked out of Detroit, Michigan. That was different. I had never been to Detroit before, and it was definitely a learning experience. When I went to Detroit, I was just recently divorced, and I had custody of my three daughters. I had a lot of support and help from my parents. My mother and father came out there, and they took turns helping us. As a single parent, it was rough. But I'm not making excuses. I never

Dan Moon, terminal superintendent at Norfolk Southern's Oliver Yard, New Orleans, 2006. *Norfolk Southern Corporation.*

heard anybody make excuses. My grandfather didn't make any excuses. My parents didn't make any excuses. And making excuses just wasn't in my vocabulary. So we made do. And with the support of my family, we made it. I'm very happy. I've raised three daughters, two of whom have already graduated from college, and my youngest is a junior in college.

My grandfather passed away in 1980, right before I graduated from high school. He didn't get the opportunity to see me work for the railroad, but I think about it every time I run the engine. I think about my grandfather because I know he would have been really proud to have seen that. I think about my grandfather and his days of going to work, and I think about some of the things he went through. I was working as a conductor—they weren't even allowed to do that. So that was already a big thing. And then to go to engineering school—that was like a dream for them. That was big. Working for the railroad makes me feel proud because I am connected with my grandfather. I know how he carried himself, and this is my chance to walk in his footsteps. I try to make the best of it.

Chapter 12
MIKE WORRELL

Mike Worrell, 2013. *Photo by Art Sellers.*

Michael (Mike) W. Worrell was born in Roanoke in 1973. Although he attended integrated schools, his family was the first African American family to move into his northwest Roanoke neighborhood. He attended Concord University in Athens, West Virginia, and was hired as a conductor for Norfolk Southern in 1996. He was promoted to locomotive engineer in 1998 and became the first African American engineer on the Roanoke Division. He comes from a railroad family. Mr. Worrell's uncle Kester Blackwell is an engineer for NS and has over forty years of service. His wife's grandfather Thurman Foy retired from N&W as a foreman in the material yard and held many other jobs with the railroad in his long career. Mr. Worrell is one of the founders of Rails of Color and the CABOOSE after-school program.

NORFOLK SOUTHERN

"You don't have to like me, but you will respect me."

It was Norfolk Southern at the time. I woke up one morning and looked at the paper. I said, "Well, I'll give this a shot and see if I get hired." I said, "If I get hired, I'll go to work. If not, I'll go back to school." And I got hired. It was in August 1996, and I got hired and started my railroad career.

I was hired as a conductor, and it was interesting. When I first started as a conductor, I thought it was going to be a more challenging job than it turned out to be, both physically and mentally. When you say you're going to work on the railroad, I was thinking I was going to have to work hard. But I found out that it was an easier job than I realized. The conductor takes care of the train, makes sure everything goes well with the cars on the train and the cargo and keeps up with the paperwork.

I was on call. I spent the first eight months of my railroad career in Winston-Salem, North Carolina. I got forced down there to work. It was a little different because I was away from home and pretty much had to stay in a hotel for a couple months. But then I found an apartment there. Eventually, I made my way. My seniority allowed me to come back to Roanoke, and then shortly thereafter, I had to go into a locomotive school. When you get hired now, you have to accept the position to become a locomotive engineer within a certain time period or whenever your seniority says you have to. That's what the contract negotiates.

I became a locomotive engineer in August 1998. I was the first African American engineer on what is called the Roanoke District out of Roanoke, which goes from Roanoke to Shenandoah. It was challenging at first. It was a situation where I had a lot of negative things that were said to me at first. On the railroad, we have signal territory and dark territory, which you don't have signals in. On one of the first trips I made, one of the engineer's remarks was: "Now we're on a dark railroad." I looked at him and said, "Are you referring to me or the actual signals?" He said, "Whichever one it applies to." I'm not a small person in stature, and I was a lot more vocal back then than I am now. So I told him, "You don't have to like me, but you will respect me." And that's just one of the stances I took in my training as a locomotive engineer and the way I work today. I tell anybody, "You don't have to like me, and I don't have to like you. But we will respect each other."

You have to understand, being there in 1998 and being the first African American engineer—it was just something that they weren't used to. They had never had to deal with it, and if you never deal with anything, you don't have to worry about it. So it was new to them and new to me. Things got better with time. I feel as though there is still some resentment because I have good seniority there now. But overall, I think a lot of the working conditions have gotten a lot better. It's what I would call "underlying undertones" that you had to look out for. But like I said, I let people know that I'll respect you if you respect me.

One of the incidents had to go through the union and everything, but it worked out. It was a person that I considered a friend who said some things over a recorded phone call that probably could have cost him his job. We've all said things and done things that we are ashamed of, and I didn't think that it should cost him his livelihood. I told him, "I can forgive you. It's easy to forgive, but I'll never forget."

RAILS OF COLOR

"We wanted the community to know that Norfolk Southern was more than just a railroad that runs through their city."

I'd say probably four or five of us put our heads together to start Rails of Color. We wanted the community to know that Norfolk Southern was more than just a railroad that ran through their city. We were an organization that gave back to the community. So we wanted to start Rails of Color, and we started what we call the CABOOSE after-school program with a couple of schools in the Roanoke Valley. Our mission is "keeping kids on track." That was our thinking. We wanted to give back to the community some of our oral history. We wanted to give them positive male role models from throughout the railroad so they could see something positive. There are boys and girls. We have females in our organization who help us, and the name "Rails of Color" is people of all origins and backgrounds in the railroad who come together. We meet and let kids see what opportunities the railroad offers them. We let them know about Norfolk Southern. We mainly tell them they need to stay in school and continue their education and that Norfolk Southern is a good company to work for.

Donne W. Jones, Norfolk Southern's manager of instructional design for Human Resources at Norfolk headquarters, photographed at the N&W African American Heritage Celebration, where he was keynote speaker, Virginia Museum of Transportation, June 2013. *Norfolk Southern Corporation.*

EVOLUTION OF THE RAILROAD

"I've got shoes older than you."

The railroad has gotten a lot better. Times have changed. In the 1940s through the '60s, there was still segregation going on. But with time, the railroad changed just like everything else had to change. It has a lot more opportunities for African Americans and for women now. A lot has changed, and it's made it a better place to work for.

My wife's grandfather Thurman Foy worked for the railroad. He worked in the material yard as a laborer and eventually became a foreman. I want to say he started in the 1940s, and he worked up until the late 1970s. So to

African American N&W Heritage Members of the Association of Colored Trainmen and Locomotive Firemen Inc. and the Ladies Auxiliary Association of Colored Trainmen in front of the Gainsboro Library, Roanoke, Virginia, circa 1937. Photo courtesy of the Harrison Museum of African American Culture, Roanoke. *Virginia Museum of Transportation.*

come from a laborer to a foreman—that was a big feat. As I mentioned, my uncle Kester Blackwell was very happy with the railroad. It provided a great living for him and his kids and wife, so he is very positive about it. When I did get hired, he was telling me all the opportunities I would have. He never spoke any ill of the railroad. He was very happy that they provided him with a job, and he loves his job—he really does. I think it's something that he really loves to do.

Growing up, I never thought that that's what I would end up doing. But looking back on it, it was something fun. It's fun to see the engineer riding down the track as a kid, waving at you, and now I'm that person that's doing the waving at other kids and blowing the horn. I take it for granted a lot of times. But when I go out into the public and tell people what I actually do, they say, "You should be honored to do that." And I really should be because there was a point in time that African Americans couldn't hold that job. So it's an honor, and at the same time, it's just a great job. There's never a dull moment. I think everybody takes their job for granted sometimes. I take it for granted at times, but when I really sit back and look at it, and when I talk to kids or different organizations and I tell them what I do and see their faces light up, then I can appreciate my job a lot more.

At the Heritage Group, you go in and listen to their stories. You sit back, and it's their time. And when we go in there, we let them tell us their stories—like Mr. Holland saying that he started making forty cents an hour and how much he made and what he did. Just to know that he started off as a laborer—and I would have never known that—and ended up as a manager of tariffs…just to know that and to see the smile on his face makes your day. And then you listen to Mr. Swain. He comes in, and he's the bitter side of it. He's telling you the stories of why he left the railroad. But it's all in fun. It lets me know why I'm at where I'm at today. Without those guys laying the road, there would be a lot of people who wouldn't be in the position they are in today—African Americans, women, Latinos, a lot of different people. You look at the railroad now, and we have Latinos, African Americans, Asian Indians and American Indians. It's a broad spectrum of different people.

I was taught from an early age to sit back and listen. And if you listen, you learn a lot through their stories. I mean, some of them are a little fabricated and a little far out, but their stories mean so much to them. And it's something that I'll be able to tell my kids about—how I got here because of what they've done. Listening to them, some days can be a little boring, but other days it's very interesting because they are such a wealth of knowledge. There's history and knowledge in those people that you can't read in a book. You can't get it anywhere else. Everybody needs to hear it because not only is it a story of them, it's actually a story of the railroad and how they got to where they're at. Without their stories, there wouldn't be an America anywhere—it wouldn't be anything. Those are the people who paved the way for a lot of different people.

These gentlemen down at the Transportation Museum—they are the ones who had these long illustrious forty-year careers, and they have stories to tell for days. For me, with the railroad…it's been interesting. Seventeen years is not short, but compared to the other guys you've interviewed, I'm a baby. And I tell them that all the time. I say, "I'm just a baby." Mr. Holland has told me several times, "I've got shoes older than you."

Afterword
African American Traditions and the Railroad

Folklore is the name for all of the traditional materials (from songs, stories and jokes to costumes, rituals and recipes) passed along informally (usually by word of mouth or demonstrated example) among groups of people, and a group that passes folklore along is called a folk group. The first folk group to which anyone belongs is the family. And as one grows older, he or she can belong to many folk groups simultaneously. Folk groups based on gender, race, religion, nationality or geographical region are but the most obvious. One of the earliest folk groups identified by professional folklorists, and one that continues to draw the attention of folklore collectors, is the occupational folk group.

The traditions of railroad workers, their folklore, have long been recognized and studied by collectors of folklore. We all, folklorists or not, recognize the railroad worker's costume: denim bib-front overalls, a work shirt (often gray), black steel-toe boots and a denim cap. We know folk songs that have come to us from railroad events: "John Henry," "Wreck of the Old '97," various songs about the New Market Train Wreck and others. We know less about the jokes they told, the initiation rituals for new workers, the informal terms they had for the tools of their trade, the people with whom they worked and the elements of the job itself.

Perhaps the most popular subjects for study over the years have been the "gandy dancers," those crews of men who laid new track and maintained existing track with shovels, pry bars, sledgehammers and other hand tools. Most of that work is now done by machines, the "steam drill" having beaten

John Henry, as it were. But there are still small crews working here and there throughout the United States. That hard manual labor has been documented in films like *Gandy Dancers 1973* and *Gandy Dancers*. *Gandy Dancers 1973* is a fourteen-minute film by Thomas G. Burton and Jack Schrader that shows an actual crew at work and records the songs that helped workers coordinate the strenuous work of rail alignment. The film shows men driving spikes with sledgehammers and then cuts to a short clip of a mechanical spike driver. There is also a brief scene in which we hear a porter going through his instructions to passengers as a train pulls into Johnson City, Tennessee. *Gandy Dancers* is a thirty-minute film made in 1994 by Barry Dornfeld and Maggie Holtzberg-Call. This film includes archival footage and black-and-white photographs, as well as interviews with and re-creations of work by retired railroad men who discuss the work songs and chants as ways of coordinating heavy work, as a means to uplift spirits and as outlets for criticisms of the "bosses" (their immediate foremen). The interviewees talk about the availability of promotions as the unions and civil rights legislation eliminated long-standing racial barriers, and they also talk about railroad men as the pride of the community, as the steady pay allowed them to dress well, buy houses and send their children to college.

Another widely recognized black railroad worker, and one whose group has been studied by folklorists, is the Pullman porter. The 1983 film *Miles of Smiles, Years of Struggle*, produced by Paul Wagner and Jack Santino, and Jack Santino's 1991 book, *Miles of Smiles, Years of Struggle: Stories of Black Pullman Porters*, document the work of the Pullman porters and the struggle, between 1925 and 1937, of those men to establish the Brotherhood of Sleeping Car Porters, the first black trade union and an important part of the civil rights movement of the 1950s and '60s. These interviewees, too, talk about the post-unionized porters being able to dress well, buy houses and send their children to college.

This book, *African American Railroad Workers of Roanoke: Oral Histories of the Norfolk and Western*, focuses on the stories of African American men and women from Roanoke, Virginia, who worked for the Norfolk & Western, now Norfolk Southern, from the late 1930s to the present day. The interviews were done to document the contributions of an under-recognized community of workers in what was and still is a major railroad hub in southwestern Virginia. The African American Heritage Group of Norfolk and Western employees and other members of the community, including the Virginia Museum of Transportation and the Historical Society of Western Virginia, have been trying to find a way to fund this project for some time. Now, having found some local funding and added a grant from the Virginia Foundation for the Humanities, the project to expand the archives with more extensive interviews and produce this book, based on those interviews, is a reality.

While the interviews for this book were not done to collect on-the-job elements of folk speech or examples of jokes, initiation rituals, songs, pranks or the like, some hints of the existence of those things appear from time to time. Clinton Scott talks about being teased because of his size when he was sent to do heavy work in the Wheel Shop: "We [the Wheel Shop foremen] sent for horses, and they sent ponies." He further explains that the yard foreman who sent him and the Wheel Shop foreman to whom he reported did not get along. David Cobbs, now an assistant vice-president for Diversity and Equal Employment Opportunity, remembers being totally worn out after his first day on a track gang. He was thinking that might be his last day until someone said to him, "I guess whoever has you is going to win the pool." Realizing that there was betting on who would stay and who would be the first to quit strengthened Cobbs's resolve to stay on the job. Both the teasing of Scott and the betting on Cobbs are the sorts of practices that can be found, especially on all-male work sites, from the railroads and the steel mills to the oil rigs and the deep woods.

A workplace usually has its own distinctive language, especially an informal language or set of terms not found in the organization's official publications but a common language developed and handed down from worker to worker. Claude James Page III says at one point that he didn't like being a supervisor and "went back to my tools." He then explained to interviewer Sheree Scarborough that "tools" are like qualifications and that because he had an engineering license, he could go back to running an engine. He also comments that some of the managers coming out of college did not have any "tools," i.e., qualifications to do anything else on the railroad. John Nutter talks about being an engineer, running an engine and liking that job; he also talks about "closet fans," men who became engineers because of "their fascination with the railroad." On another level of folk speech, Brenda Powell mentions the language she heard as a woman in a previously all-male situation. She comments that "some of it was foul, but none of it was ever—at least not around me—women-related." She further states, "It was just the language that came out of their mouths," acknowledging that these men had developed an on-the-job language among themselves before there were women on the job and that they occasionally slipped into that language in her presence and then apologized for it: "Oh, excuse me, I didn't mean for that to come out." (I know from my own experience working on the railroad that such men did not take that language home with them at the end of the day.)

While hints of such traditional folk elements exist throughout the interviews, what comes out most strongly is the sense of community that pervades these narratives. Many of the interviewees mention that they grew up in a close-knit neighborhood. To some extent, the neighborhood was a close-knit one because African Americans at that time were only allowed to live in certain neighborhoods, and within those neighborhoods were African American–owned businesses, providing both necessities (such as groceries and prescription medicines) and entertainment (such as movies and live performances). It is important to note, for the purposes of this book, that the major African American neighborhood in Roanoke was near the railroad yards. Several of the interviewees mention watching the trains, often from the Henry Street Bridge, when they were youngsters. John Nutter comments, "Well, I spent a lot of time watching trains. My haunts were the Henry Street Bridge and the Fifth Street Bridge, and when I could get away with it, I would walk down to the station…and watch the trains."

Children like John Nutter not only watched the trains, they also watched their fathers go off to work every day for the railroad. In many cases, working for the railroad became a family occupation. Robert E. Hamlin recounts his father's employment on various railroads before he came to work at the Norfolk & Western and discusses his own route to becoming a railroad worker. Phillip Randolph says, " Just about my whole family that I know of…worked on the railroad" and adds that his own son is now working there. Claude James Page III comments that his father did not work for the railroad but that working for the railroad helped him connect with his railroader grandfather, who had: "I know he would have been really proud of me."

J.R. Hughes, whose father also worked for the railroad, feels that the African American families of railroad workers were very stable in those days, partly because of the steady income and partly because of the importance of the church in their lives. The railroad provided not only the vertical connection between family members of different generations but also a horizontal connection among members of the community. Dyke M. Wood explains that everybody knew everybody else within a three- or four-block radius and that "if I cut up two blocks over, I would get disciplined [there] before I got home to the real discipline. It was ok with my parents, and I knew that."

During that time, railroad men were held in high esteem—and held themselves in high esteem. John Nutter remembers that when you talked to railroad men, "you always got the feeling that they were extremely proud of working for the railroad...If you worked anywhere else, you didn't have a job." The other thing that he says made an impression on him was "the way they looked." As some of the photographs in this book indicate, the railroad men were always well dressed when they were off the job and out in public. Nutter continues, "Yes, the jobs may have been in service, but they were always sharp—shoes shined, clothes neatly pressed—and they carried themselves in a very distinct way." J.R. Hughes remembers, "Those men gave us—railroad men's children—a certain dignity. They gave us a cut in our strut because they demanded that you acted like somebody."

Civil rights legislation, changes in cultural attitudes, widening economic opportunities and technological advances have greatly changed the physical, geographic community in which these interviewees grew up and in which they came to understand what the railroad meant in their lives. But the spirit of that community lives on—not only in the memories of the workers and former workers who gave these interviews but also in their commitment to a now larger community. Two programs, Rails of Color and CABOOSE, were begun by members of the N&W African American Heritage Group. CABOOSE, as its name cleverly implies, is an after-school program whose mission is to "keep the kids on track." Rails of Color is a mentoring program that attempts to provide positive role models to kids from all groups, regardless of race or gender. Mike Worrell, one of the co-founders, explains, "I wanted the community to know that Norfolk Southern was more than just a railroad that ran through their city. We were an organization that gave back to the community."

C.W. Sullivan III, PhD
Emeritus Professor of English
East Carolina University

Afterword

AFRICAN AMERICAN RAILROADERS
IN THE ROANOKE VALLEY

The contributions of African American employees of the old Norfolk & Western Railway and the new Norfolk Southern are immeasurable. So many of them started at the bottom, cleaning floors and spittoons, and slowly worked their way upward into jobs based on merit rather than race.

Their persistence through thick and thin has been gathered in part through an oral history program at the Virginia Museum of Transportation, an oral history project funded in part by the Historical Society of Western Virginia and now that has been expanded into this illustrated book, *African American Railroad Workers of Roanoke: Oral Histories of the Norfolk and Western*, scheduled for publication by summer of 2014. Al Holland, the ninety-seven-year-old leader of the project, explains the symbolism of the title of the oral history project, "Cotton to Silk: Oral Histories of African American Workers of the Norfolk & Western," when he talks about his forty-six years on the N&W: "It was the best job I could get because the steel mill wasn't paying as much as the railroad was. There wasn't any other outfit paying as much as the railroad for labor, and that's what I would be getting, a laboring job. I went with the railroad. I stayed with the railroad…We took what we could get, and we made a life for ourselves…We made cotton, but we took that cotton and made silk…We had to take what we had down here because we weren't going to get those jobs."

Recalling that he started as a janitor and worked up to assistant manager, Holland said the next generation went through training, and they were hired as engineers and conductors. His father, Gus Holland, a railroad blacksmith, never owned a car and walked to work. Al Holland started at N&W at thirty-eight cents an hour in the days when a loaf of bread cost "a nickel or a dime."

Holland, Roanoke's Citizen of the Year in 2003, has been a model of community service, from fifty years as a scoutmaster to his work in many civic and church organizations, in addition to his day job. Always in good humor, he's a friend of many of us in both black and white communities.

Most of us in the community have watched the trains roll by over the years, carrying coal and increasingly varied loads of chemicals and industrial products, and some of us have been fortunate to own a few shares of N&W stock, but we have had little understanding of the work force that made this possible in what was recognized as "a railroad town" for many years. Segregation was a fact of life, a mindset that saw no wrong in saving the best jobs for everybody except African Americans.

The life stories of these strong-willed people have been recorded for the book by oral historian Sheree Scarborough, who talked with and edited the recollections and observations of more than twenty mainly elderly, retired railroad veterans. These interviews open a window into the lives of men, mainly across the tracks in the northwest section of Roanoke, who have played a major role in keeping the trains running. A grant from the Virginia Foundation for the Humanities to the Historical Society of Western Virginia made the project possible. Scarborough is a Texas native living in Floyd County who has more than thirty years of oral history experience. The historical society is pleased to offer this glimpse into a segment of Roanoke's industrial community, largely overlooked for more than 140 years.

As they are able, these old railroaders meet monthly at the Virginia Museum of Transportation to exchange memories and reflect on changing times at the merged Norfolk Southern Railway. A few current or recent employees add to the conversation. Their recollections provide invaluable information about the work climate of African Americans on the tracks and in the yards and offices for future generations.

Importantly, one woman told of her experience. Brenda Powell, who is still working as a programmer in the IT department, said most African Americans in N&W offices were messengers or outside unloading trains and performing heavy labor when she started in 1978. The company was "pretty much an all-male environment...women were slowly coming into [it] because most were secretaries or clerks." She began as management in the IT department, but her father was a railroad baggage handler.

Norfolk Southern has three African American vice-presidents today. David Cobbs, an assistant vice-president for diversity and equal opportunity employment, spent a summer laying track but after college took a management job and started in Buffalo, New York, where he was the only black employee in the yard. Today, he told the *Roanoke Times*, "The railroad is a microcosm of society," and in terms of employee diversity, "I don't think there's a glass ceiling per se anymore."

Cobbs, elected president of the student body at Patrick Henry High School in Roanoke in the second year after integration, remembered tension and friction when the races were integrated. His parents and other relatives cautioned him with advice: "Be careful around those people over there. Don't do anything to embarrass us when you go over there." He said court-ordered integration "wasn't a popular decision among students or among a lot of people, but there were no riots or anything like that...I think the teachers and the administrators were more on edge than the students were during that time."

After John Nutter served in the air force and drove a truck for several years, he was hired as a railroad brakeman and worked his way up to engineer. He loved trains as a boy, and when he told his mother he wanted to be an engineer, "she just looked at me like it broke her heart because at the time, a black man couldn't be an engineer." On certain jobs, he said, "the color of your skin dictated that you could not have it. And it wasn't just blacks. There's been discrimination against Irish, the Chinese and American Indians. So we're not alone in this, and I seriously doubt that we will ever have a perfectly healthy society unless everybody just becomes all mixed up."

Nutter has a good memory and provided colorful descriptions of his early interest in trains. He remembers riding a train from Lynchburg to Norfolk as a boy—"the wisp of smoke floating by and line posts looking like a picket fence." He liked to stand on the Henry (First, NW) Street and Fifth Street Bridges in Roanoke and watch the trains roll by, especially the big steam engines, which had "more personality. The thump and noises of the air compressor, the hissing from steam jackets and the pop-off valves—you could even hear the clinkers dropping from the firebox... Now, when we realize how massive those pieces of equipment were, we just take it for granted." Nutter also has clear recollections of hearing men walking to work in the East End Shops from his northeast neighborhood at about six-thirty in the morning to start work at seven. "You could hear the tramp of feet as those men walked to the shops."

Carroll Swain, an N&W freight handler and commissary worker before military service, said the main reason he left the railroad was his parents' advice: "Don't let anybody walk on you." This was "quite difficult for me.

I just couldn't make it," he added. Swain rose to lieutenant colonel in the army, served in Vietnam and later worked for Roanoke City Schools and served on the city council. He recalled that his father, Robert Swain, was a coach cleaner on N&W for thirty-nine years, never earning more than $100 a month. His father once worked two jobs—as a freight handler five hours a day and then another eight hours in the coach yard. His uncle John Canty rolled seven-hundred-pound wheels around the railroad shops.

"Blacks had skills that could produce better things for the railroad, but the opportunity was not there for them because they had you in a class where you were employed, and you stayed that way," Swain said. "You were not promoted. That was bad." Sometimes a black trained a white person who was promoted, "and you had to say 'sir' to him" although "you knew that he didn't know any more than you know about the job."

J.R. Hughes said he was hired as the first black machinist on the N&W because "the Civil Rights Act got me my job." His father, a train porter, would come home from work "sometimes totally frustrated because some little Caucasian kid whose daddy had got him a job on the railroad would have to come to my father to learn how to be my father's boss." The N&W "wouldn't let black men become conductors in those days. Train porters, brakemen, the lowest jobs—those were the jobs that black men could get." Hughes said his father "wasn't a bitter man, but he was affected by it…This young kid, because of the color of his skin, my father had to train him to be his supervisor." Both Hughes and his father were weekend preachers.

These old-timers often worked extra hours to support large families. John Divers, a dining car cook, remembered that he cut grass and washed windows in summer and shoveled snow in winter. "In the night, I got through so I could get over to Booker T. [School] and get that cleaned up before eleven o'clock so I could go over to GE and help clean the lights at night. You had to wash the lights off at night."

Lee Graves started as a dishwasher and was promoted to chef, where he cooked in a business car for four N&W presidents: R.H. Smith, Stuart Saunders, Herman Pevler and John Fishwick. "We had some tough presidents and some good ones," he said. "They weren't hard to work for." When it came to food, Saunders was "very classy. He had a little more taste."

Terry Evans, a North Carolina Central University graduate who moved to Roanoke as a management trainee, rose to vice-president of Norfolk Southern in twenty-three years. In that service, he "probably had eighteen relocations, transfers and temporary" assignments. As an African American, he had no minority role models. "We were first," he said.

Somewhere in his busy career, he faced discrimination, "but I didn't worry about it because I've always sensed it was their problem, not mine. I found that persistence and good job performance trumps that kind of stuff [racial discrimination]." Now vice-president of transportation, a key executive position, his job is "to run the trains as hard and fast and safe as I can."

Evans is optimistic about the railroad's future workforce, noting, "More diversity is a natural progression of things."

George Kegley
Editor, Historical Society of Western Virginia *Journal*

"Days of Steam," colored pencil drawing by self-taught African American artist David Ramey. *Collection of the artist.*

EPILOGUE

As I complete this manuscript in the dead of night, just days ahead of my deadline, I've learned that the second of the narrators for this project—John W. Divers—has died. Mr. Divers was ninety-six years old and told me he had lived a good life. But I am saddened that both he and Reverend Carl Tinsley, who died last year at the age of eighty, have died before this book could get to press. Mr. Divers shared a poignant vignette in his interview that I heard in different variations in some of the other interviews as well. It is the image of the train going by and his waving. Many others remembered waving to the train as children and having their waves returned, and they spoke about waving from the train as engineers and conductors today.

I would always stand on the hill behind the house. The railroad track ran behind it. I would always stand out there when I was cutting grass. When the cars would go by, especially the passenger train, the guys—a cook or somebody—would be standing in the door in the diner waving. I waved back, and I used to think, "I wonder where they are going."
—*John Divers, March 13, 2013*

Sheree Scarborough
March 30, 2014

Appendix 1

Interviews Conducted for the Cotton to Silk Oral History Project

Cobbs, R. David—July 10, 2013
Divers, John W.—March 13, 2013
Evans, Terry N.—July 5, 2013
Graves, Lee P.—March 13, 2013
Hamlin, Robert E.—July 1, 2013
Holland, Alphonzo L.—February 15, 2013
Hughes, Junious R.—March 15, 2013
Johnson, Joseph C.—July 2, 2013
Lawrence, William M.—May 21, 2013
Mease, John R.—June 11, 2013
Nutter, John A.—June 26, 2013
Page, Claude James III—June 26, 2013
Powell, Brenda A.—July 6, 2013
Randolph, Philip A.—June 21, 2013
Scott, Clinton D.—May 14, 2013
Swain, Carroll E.—March 19, 2013
Tinsley, Carl T.—April 24, 2013
Washington, Paul B.—June 10, 2013
Wood, Dyke M.—June 28, 2013
Worrell, Michael W.—July 3, 2013

Appendix II

LIST OF DECEASED RAILROAD WORKERS ON THE NORFOLK & WESTERN IN THE ROANOKE VALLEY

(Editor's note: This list is incomplete, but I thought it would be useful to include it. It is derived from biographical data forms collected by the N&W African American Heritage Group.)

Burks, James W., Jr. (1938–2009)
Thirty-two years of service, management

Cannady, Billy, Sr. (1927–2003)
Fifteen years of service, car cleaner

Clark, Samuel H., Sr. (1885–1979)
Fifty-one-plus years of service, laborer/Pullman porter/yard brakeman

Clements, William, Sr. (1904–1979)
Forty-plus years of service, passenger car cleaner

DeBerry, William Thomas, Sr. (1916–1970)
Twenty years of service, dining car server

Ford, Sylvester G. (1922–2011)
Dining Car Department/laborer

Gunn, Tom (unknown–1939)
Twenty-five-plus years of service, storehouse worker

Hamlin, James, Jr. (1920–1995)
Twenty-one years of service, Maintenance of Way laborer

Holland, Gus (1887–1964)
Thirty-plus years of service, laborer/blacksmith

Johnson, William C. (1916–2006)
Twenty years of service, cook

Long, George Robert (1922–2001)
Twenty years of service, laborer in the East End Shops

Meadow, Luther Henry (early 1900s–1960)
Wheel Shop

Page, Claude James, Sr. (1900–1980)
Forty-eight years of service, laborer in the East End Shops

Petty, Percy (circa 1887–circa 1950)
Twenty years of service, maintenance worker

Powell, Herman C. (1924–2001)
Thirty-eight years of service, various laborer positions, including baggage handler and Red Cap

Randolph, Ulysses (1920–2011)
Thirty-nine years of service, turntable operator/laborer

Robinson, Eugene (1918–1973)
Thirty-two years of service, assistant boilermaker

Rogers, George E. (1919–2008)
Twenty-three-plus years of service, Dining Car Department

Scott, George (1880–1961)
Thirty-seven years of service, janitor

Scott, George Leon, Jr. (1919–2003)
Thirty-nine years of service, janitor in Motive Power Building

Shears, Edward H., Sr. (1936–1991)
Crane operator in the East End Shops

Smith, Joseph B. (1919–2000)
Track laborer/laborer in the East End Shops

Stovall, King S. (1918–2007)
Thirty-one years of service, Dining Car Department/brakeman/
material management

Swain, Robert Gilmore, Sr. (1897–1957)
Thirty-nine years of service, coach cleaner

Taborn, William Walter, Sr. (1881–1974)
Sixty-four years of service, Red Cap

Terrell, Glen, W. (1875–1940)
Laborer/foreman

Wallace, Eddie, Sr.
Thirty years of service, laborer

Washington, Billips Calvin (1890–1964)
Forty years of service, brakeman

Selected Bibliography

Arnesen, Eric. *Brotherhoods of Color: Black Railroad Workers and the Struggle for Equality*. Cambridge, MA: Harvard University Press, 2001.

Dotson, Rand. *Roanoke, Virginia, 1882–1912: Magic City of the New South*. Knoxville: University of Tennessee Press, 2007.

Frisch, Michael. *A Shared Authority: Essays on the Craft and Meaning of Oral and Public History*. Albany: State University of New York Press, 1990.

Harris, Nelson. *Norfolk and Western Railway*. Charleston, SC: Arcadia Publishing, 2003.

Harris, Nelson, and Harold McLeod. *Roanoke Valley*. Charleston, SC: Arcadia Publishing, 2010.

Kornweibel, Theodore, Jr. *Railroads in the African American Experience: A Photographic Journey*. Baltimore, MD: Johns Hopkins University Press, 2010.

Perata, David D. *Those Pullman Blues: An Oral History of the African American Railroad Attendant*. New York: Twayne Publishers, 1996.

Santino, Jack. *Miles of Smiles, Years of Struggle: Stories of Black Pullman Porters.* Champaign: University of Illinois Press, 1991.

Striplin, E.F. Pat. *The Norfolk & Western: A History.* Forest, VA: Norfolk & Western Historical Society Inc., 1997.

INDEX

About the Author

Sheree Scarborough is an award-winning historian with thirty years experience in oral and public history. She holds degrees (a BA, magna cum laude, and an MA) from the University of Texas at Austin, where she has done graduate work beyond the master's degree level. She has worked with various institutions over the course of her career, including the NASA/Johnson Space Center, the Library of Congress and the University of Texas School of Law. Scarborough  directed the Frank Erwin Oral History Project in the 1990s in Austin that produced an archive of over two hundred interviews with state and national leaders and has been involved in such projects as the University of Texas Oral History Project and the Pennzoil-Texaco Oral History Project. She has written or edited numerous publications in the field of oral history and other areas as well. Scarborough moved to the Blue Ridge Mountains in Virginia in 2010. Since then, she has been involved in an oral history project with the University of Virginia and most recently has conducted the interviews for and directed the Cotton to Silk Oral History Project in Roanoke.